W9-BJF-684

Slushed!

More Than 150 Frozen, Boozy Treats

for the Coolest Happy Hour Ever

JESSIE CROSS

Plus Intoxicating Ice Cream Sandwiches!

adamsmedia

Avon, Massachusetts

Published by Adams Media,
a division of F+W Media, Inc.
57 Littlefield Street, Avon, MA 02322. U.S.A.
www.adamsmedia.com

ISBN 10: 1-4405-3218-4
ISBN 13: 978-1-4405-3218-4
eISBN 10: 1-4405-3345-8
eISBN 13: 978-1-4405-3345-7

Printed in the United States of America.

10   9   8   7   6   5   4   3   2   1

Library of Congress Cataloging-in-Publication Data
is available from the publisher.

This publication is designed to provide accurate and authoritative information with regard to the subject matter covered. It is sold with the under-
standing that the publisher is not engaged in rendering legal, accounting,
or other professional advice. If legal advice or other expert assistance is
required, the services of a competent professional person should be sought.
—From a *Declaration of Principles* jointly adopted
by a Committee of the American Bar Association and
a Committee of Publishers and Associations

Many of the designations used by manufacturers and sellers to distinguish
their product are claimed as trademarks. Where those designations appear
in this book and Adams Media was aware of a trademark claim, the designations have been printed with initial capital letters.

Photo copyright by Jessie Cross.

This book is available at quantity discounts for bulk purchases.
For information, please call 1-800-289-0963.

For my wolf pack.

Acknowledgments

First and foremost, huge thanks to Edward Cross, who is not only my husband, but also my editor, business manager, resident bartender, photo stylist extraordinaire, and all-around partner in crime. I couldn't have done this without you.

Thanks to the good folks from SeeMyDrink .com for the equipment loan and expert photography advice. May your business be wildly successful!

Thanks to Andrea Hakanson, my editor at Adams, for all the input, support, and quick responses to my rapid-fire e-mails.

Thanks to my friends and tasting crew here in Salem, who gave me some wild flavor ideas and valiantly sampled their way through the good, the bad, and the ugly as I developed recipes. For my two favorite Vikings, I owe you a couple of quarts of mead ice cream. Thanks especially to a mischievous pair of little black kittens, who dragged me to the ocean, took me to the tavern for drinks, and indulged in late-night omelet dinners and cartoons when I needed to take a break.

Thanks to Cassie Bagshaw, Kristyn Ferretti, Kristin Green, Nicole Knobloch, Lori Levin, Teresa Niedzwiecki, Jennifer Novak, Christina Poteet, Kate Vassos—and all of The Hungry Mouse's readers and Facebook fans—for the cocktail inspiration. You guys may just have a second career in bartending. (Well, except for Terri. You're already the best bartender in Boston.)

Thanks to David Zubkoff, John Colbert, and Julie de Chantal for just generally being awesome.

Last but not least, extra special thanks to Lori Bruno, who saw this coming and who helped me find the will inside to get it done. Your support and encouragement mean the world to me.

I love you guys. May your homes always be filled with happiness. May your cups always be full.

+Jessie Cross
Salem, Massachusetts

Contents

Chapter 7

Granita. 103

Chapter 8

Sorbet and Sherbet 113

Chapter 9

Ice Cream Sandwiches, Cakes, and Other Frozen Novelties 129

Chapter 10

Frozen Cocktails, Milkshakes, and Smoothies **143**

Chapter 11

Toppings and Treats **153**

Introduction

The best present I ever received from my husband was a cherry-red ice cream maker for Valentine's Day seven years ago. I'm a sucker for a good piece of kitchen equipment, and it was definitely love at first sight.

Since then, I've been an ice cream–making machine! Add to that my love of cocktails and fine spirits, and I have a serious addiction to blending booze with dessert. The best part is creating new recipes, trying new flavors, and seeing what works well together.

Two scoops of Boozy Brazilian Chocolate Truffle Ice Cream drizzled with homemade hot fudge sauce? A dish of Chocolate Frangelico Gelato dotted with toasted hazelnuts? An extra-thick vanilla shake fragrant with maple and bourbon? Miniature Molasses and Ginger Brandy Ice Cream Sandwiches? Yes, please!

Adding alcohol to ice cream and her chilly cousins is one of those great acts of culinary alchemy. The result is one part dessert, one part cocktail. The trick is getting the proportions just right. Too much alcohol and your ice cream won't freeze. Too little, and your flavor can fall flat.

This book is your guide to making frozen desserts spiked with your favorite liquors. We'll cover all the basics—with a boozy twist.

Is chocolate ice cream your favorite? Let's deepen the flavor with a little chocolate liqueur and a shot of espresso vodka. How about that blackberry smoothie you get at the gym? Blend in some Limoncello and serve it in champagne flutes at your next movie night, topped with a splash of Prosecco.

We'll make liqueur-infused sorbets, granitas, and frozen ice pops—not to mention milkshakes and frozen cocktails. You'll also find a handful of treats and toppings at the end to round out the dessert extravaganza. (Hello, Frozen Kahlua Cheesecake!)

Never made ice cream before? It's really no sweat. There's (practically) nothing to it. You'll be a pro in no time. You just need to learn a few basic techniques, like how to make a custard without curdling it, what ingredients are better suited for sorbets than ice cream, and what to use if you don't have a spiffy, cherry-red ice cream machine. The most important thing to remember is this: Cook with all your senses. Including common sense. In my kitchen, recipes are a guideline. How firm or loose is up to you.

Squeeze your produce. (Is it ripe?) Taste absolutely everything, from those peaches (are they bursting with flavor?) to that mint extract (how strong is it, anyway?). Trust your taste buds, and don't be afraid to substitute or improvise if you hit a few bumps. Nibble on that licorice. (Is it a little on the hard side? Cut it into extra-small pieces.) Look at your finished product. (Is the color appealing? Would it be happier with a sauce or a handful of nuts mixed in for texture?)

If you like it, chances are your guests will, too. And if a recipe sounds great, but includes one ingredient you can't stand, don't be afraid to find a substitution and alter a recipe to suit your tastes. (Love spicy, spiked coffee but hate the idea of tequila in the Mexican Coffee Sorbet? Try substituting Kahlua or coffee brandy.)

So, what's better? A big bowl of creamy, luscious ice cream or a tall, frozen cocktail? Put them together in an epic act of culinary alchemy and a third super treat emerges: The Booze-Infused Frozen Dessert.

Welcome to Slushed!

Chapter 1

Getting Down to Basics: Technique, Equipment, and Ingredients

You might think that making ice cream is a long, tedious process that just seems like too much work. Why make it at home when you can grab a cone at your local ice cream shop or a pint of Ben & Jerry's at the store? But making ice cream isn't nearly as scary or difficult as you might think. Nothing beats the taste of homemade ice cream, and you can create any flavor you want. The best part? Your ice cream maker will do most of the hard work for you. There are just a couple of things you need to know before you get started.

Technique

Ice cream falls into two basic categories: Custard-based and Philadelphia-style. They're made a little differently but both are absolutely delicious.

Custard-Based Ice Cream

Custard-based ice cream starts out with a cooked egg custard. It's rich and delicious. This is the stuff that most Americans think of when they think of ice cream. It involves babysitting a mixture of egg yolks, milk, and cream on the stove to be sure that it gets nice and thick—but doesn't separate into a curdle-y mess.

Sound difficult? It doesn't have to be. You just need to know a little bit about the science behind custard cookery. A lot of ice cream recipes will tell you to cook the custard until it's thick enough to coat the back of a spoon. That's well and fine for

veteran ice creamieres, but that's a pretty general statement if you've never done it before.

The trick to making foolproof ice cream is to use a candy thermometer when you cook the custard. The magic number for ice cream and gelato is 170°F. That's hot enough to ensure that the eggs are properly cooked—but not so high that you wind up with an icky pot of scrambled eggs (which starts to happen around 180°F). Other key things to know: always use a heavy-bottomed pot over medium heat, never high. And don't ever, ever let the custard boil (which happens around 212°F, which you'll never reach because you're using a candy thermometer).

Don't Sweat the Custard Seriously. Making ice cream isn't rocket science—and it's not the end of the world if you accidentally curdle your custard. If you try something and it doesn't work out, just toss it, take a deep breath, and start again. If you're new to making ice cream, start with simple, inexpensive ingredients, just in case. The first time I tried to make ice cream, I think I made six batches before I got it right.

Philadelphia-Style Ice Cream

The other main kind of ice cream is known as Philadelphia-style ice cream, which skips the custard altogether. Philly-style is made from a simpler, uncooked mixture of cream, sugar, and flavorings. There are no eggs at all. Basically, you mix all your ingredients together in a bowl, chill it, then process it in your ice cream maker. Pretty simple, eh?

Equipment

When making ice cream, you'll need fairly standard kitchen equipment for the most part. Think 3- to 4-quart saucepans, frying pans, mixing bowls, baking dishes, sheet pans, measuring cups and spoons, knives, a strainer, a whisk, a zester, a veggie peeler, wooden spoons, spatulas, and so forth.

A little electric scale is nice to have for measuring out chocolate, fruit, and other ingredients.

Specialized kitchen gadgets like the ones discussed next aren't always necessary, but they'll make your life easier when you're making ice cream. That said, once you get the technique down, it's easy to be creative and improvise if you don't have a certain gadget at hand.

Ice Cream Maker

Obviously, this is the big one. There are a range of ice cream makers on the market, from low-tech insulated balls that you roll around by hand, to luxury, self-contained units with built-in compressors that produce finished ice cream in half an hour. What you buy depends on your budget, the amount of available storage space, and how long you want to wait before the ice cream is frozen.

You can snag a good-quality, electric ice cream maker for under $80 almost anywhere these days. I personally use both a 1-quart and a 2-quart Cuisinart model and absolutely love them. With most mid-range electric ice cream makers like this, you'll need to freeze the ice cream bowl ahead of time. If you have the room, store the bowl in the freezer. That way, it's ready whenever the ice cream–making mood strikes you.

Oh, and definitely take the time to read the instructions that come with your particular machine. They all work a little differently.

Blender or Food Processor

Blenders and food processors play a huge role in ice cream making. You don't necessarily need an expensive model; you just need one that works well. In many of the following recipes, you'll be cooking ingredients for an ice cream flavor base and then puréeing them. A blender or food processor can also help you purée fresh berries, chop nuts, whip cream, and so forth.

Mixer

You'll want some kind of mixer—be it a professional-grade stand mixer or your grandmother's rotary egg beater. For recipes that require a lot of heavy-duty beating, like the frozen cheesecakes or simple whipped cream, your arms will thank you if you have an electric model.

Candy Thermometer

Using a candy thermometer is one of the dirty little secrets of producing flawless custard for your ice cream. It clips to the inside of your pot, and it can help you keep from overcooking—and curdling—your custard. Just be sure it doesn't touch the bottom, or you can get a faulty reading. They're inexpensive—grab one at any home goods store.

Pop Molds

These days, you can find all sorts of pop molds. You can use standard frozen ice pop molds, or you can get creative with silicone cake/cookie/candy molds. If you're improvising, be sure to consider the final product. (Is the shape practical for eating on a stick?) If you want to go old school, paper cups still work just as well as they did when you were a kid.

Storage

You can't go wrong storing ice cream in thick, plastic, Tupperware-style containers. If you don't want to buy special containers, a standard, 1-pound bread loaf pan holds about a quart of ice cream. You'll just have to wrap it really well with plastic wrap to avoid freezer burn.

Springform Pan

If you want to make frozen cheesecakes, a springform pan is a must. This two-part cheese-cake pan has a removable outer ring, which makes serving a breeze.

Cherry Pitter

A cherry pitter is a nifty little contraption that knocks the pit right out of a cherry. It's nice to have, but not necessary. You can improvise one by punching a plastic drinking straw through ripe cherries. If you love cherries, you might want to spend a couple of bucks on a bulk cherry pitter, which can process several pounds an hour. Again, consider your needs and invest in what makes sense for you. Cherries can be a pain to pit if you have a lot to do.

Ingredients

The great thing about making your own frozen treats is that you control absolutely everything that goes into them. This is especially good for people concerned with food allergies, special diets, or organic eating. Most commercial ice creams rely on a ton of binders and stabilizers to keep their product smooth and scoopable. Always buy the highest-quality ingredients you can. Most of the recipes in this book don't have a ton of stuff in them, so every flavor will shine.

Prepared ingredients vs. 100-percent home-made ingredients is always a hot topic for debate.

The ingredients for these recipes are as simple and accessible as possible to keep the treats easy and practical to make. Don't feel like you have to make every little thing from scratch—unless you want to.

For example, some of fruit-based recipes call for jam—or bottled fruit nectar or juice—instead of cooked fresh fruit. This approach is suggested partially out of convenience for you, and partially because some fruits, like figs, are hard to find out of season, or can be time-consuming to deal with. However, if you're inclined to, by all means juice the fruit yourself, or cook the jam by hand. The finished product will be that much better for your effort. If you're itching to do that, you probably already have a pretty good idea of what you're doing.

Alcohol

Because alcohol basically doesn't freeze, it helps keep your frozen treats soft and scoopable straight out of the container. (A blessing and a curse, right? Talk about irresistible midnight snacks that don't keep you waiting.) Just remember that, with most frozen treats, more isn't necessarily better. You can only add so much booze before your ice cream won't freeze properly.

- In general, you can add ¼ cup of 80-proof liquor to about a quart of ice cream.
- For lower-proof liqueurs and cordials, you can add a little more, between ⅓ and ½ cup per quart, depending on the booze and how strong it is.
- For low-proof beer and wine, you can add about 1½ cups per quart.

As a rule, always use good-quality booze that you'd be willing to drink. If you don't like the flavor in a glass, chances are you aren't going to like it in an ice cream.

Nerd Alert For all you nerds out there, yes, technically, pure alcohol (a.k.a. ethanol) does freeze—at something like -173°F. That said, unless you have a NASA-level freezer available to you, your booze is probably never going to freeze solid in your home freezer. Of course, liqueurs with lower percentages of alcohol and other ingredients will freeze at (slightly) higher temperatures. Did you know that:

- 25-proof booze freezes around 20°F?
- 60-proof booze freezes around -10°F?
- 80-proof booze freezes around -30°F?

Coconut Milk

Coconut milk is basically juice extracted from the coconut. It adds heavenly coconut flavor to ice cream. Don't confuse it with coconut cream, which has a ton of additional sugar. Find canned coconut milk (light or regular) in the Asian section of most major grocery stores.

Coffee

For all the recipes in this book that call for coffee, use a strong roast, like French or Italian. Even if you wouldn't drink something that strong in the morning, remember that it's serving as a flavoring agent. If you're worried about caffeine, use decaf. If you don't normally make coffee at home, there's nothing wrong with running down to your local café and grabbing a cup or two to go.

Cream

Cream is categorized by how much butterfat it contains. The recipes in this book that call for heavy cream contain about 36 percent butterfat. Whipping cream is pretty much the same thing for our purposes here, so feel free to substitute if you like. For amazing flavor, try to buy your dairy products for these recipes from a local dairy.

Fat Equals Flavor In the culinary world, fat equals flavor, plain and simple. With ice cream, gelato, and frozen yogurt, you can skimp on fat—just know that you're probably compromising flavor and/or texture.

That said, this definitely isn't a diet ice cream cookbook. If you have certain dietary restrictions, by all means follow them. Just don't be surprised when the ice cream you made with no cream and nonfat milk tastes like, well, drywall compound.

Eggs

If every ingredient plays a role in a recipe, eggs are the glue. They provide form and structure, and they help hold things together. Eggs are considered safe to eat when they're cooked to 160°F. Check the temperature of custards using a candy or instant-read thermometer. Most recipes in this book call for the custard to be heated to 170°F.

> *Brown Eggs vs. White* What's the difference? Simply put, not much. The old myth that brown eggs are better is exactly that: a myth. Brown eggs come from a different breed of chicken, that's all. Inside, brown and white eggs are basically identical. Sure, you can split nutritional hairs between breeds, based on diet and other factors. But for our purposes, an egg is an egg. Plus, white eggs are almost always cheaper.

Espresso

Some of the recipes in this book call for espresso made from instant espresso powder. Buy a jar and store it in your freezer to make sure it stays fresh. Espresso acts as an instant flavor enhancer in chocolate-based ice creams (and most chocolate-based baked goods). Simply follow the recipe's instructions.

Fruit Juice

For these recipes, fruit juice means straight-up juice with no additional sugar. Make it yourself, or buy it in a carton or bottle from the store.

Fruit Nectar

Unlike fruit juice, fruit nectar includes sugar. Look for bottles that have a minimal amount of ingredients, with fruit and sugar being the first ones. To keep the results from being too sweet, in most recipes that include fruit nectar, little other sugar is added.

Milk

For all recipes that call for milk, use whole milk. Don't skimp and use skim milk or even 2%. Those both contain more water, which results in an icier, less flavorful final product.

Vanilla

Did you know that vanilla is one of the most expensive spices in the world, second only to saffron? Buy real vanilla extract—not imitation vanilla flavoring. The difference is huge. If you like, you can make your own with vanilla beans and vodka (see Chapter 11).

Yogurt

For recipes that call for yogurt, use whole milk Greek-style yogurt, which is thick, creamy, and loaded with protein. Look for yogurts with all natural ingredients, active cultures, and as few (or no) additives as possible. Keep in mind that, as with ice cream and gelato, if you use a lower fat yogurt, you're going to wind up with a much less creamy froyo.

Frozen Ice Pops

Boozy pops are like a cocktail on a stick. They're portable. They're individual. They're quite possibly the perfect frozen treat.

From old-school cherry pops to the deeply flavorful Mexican paletas that are all the rage these days, pops are a great way to cool off. Plus, you can get insanely creative with juice and booze combinations. And don't limit yourself to regular ol' wooden sticks. Try whole cinnamon sticks, sugarcane spears, rock candy sticks, sturdy cocktail stirrers, and other resourceful stand-ins. Just be sure you use something that's relatively easy to hold.

Ready to make your own? Start with your favorite cocktail recipe and adapt it using this basic ratio: 3 cups of juice or other liquid to ¼ cup alcohol to make about ten 3-ounce pops.

Fiery Chili Lime Tequila Pops

MAKES ABOUT 5 POPS

4 medium-sized cucumbers, peeled, seeded, and chopped

2 tablespoons sugar

¼ cup freshly squeezed lime juice

⅛ teaspoon ground chipotle chili powder

3 tablespoons tequila

Two words: *frozen fire*. A pinch of ground chipotle chili powder and a generous pour of tequila give these pops enough heat to make you blush. Puréed cucumber is an unexpected—but very refreshing—base for these icy, Mexican-style treats. Fresh lime juice brightens up the flavor and adds a little sass.

1. Purée the cucumbers in a food processor or blender until smooth. Strain the purée into a large bowl.
2. Add the sugar, lime juice, chipotle chili powder, and tequila. Whisk until the sugar completely dissolves.
3. Pour into pop molds, leaving ¼ inch at the top. Freeze until slushy, then insert a stick into each. Freeze overnight, until solid.

Too Hot to Handle? For less heat but plenty of chili flavor, use regular vodka and a milder chili powder, like ancho, poblano, or Anaheim.

Serving Tips Because they're barely sweet, these aren't your typical dessert pops. Serve them alongside (or instead of) appetizers at a steamy summer barbecue.

Cosmo Pops

MAKES 8-10 POPS

2½ cups 100% cranberry juice

½ cup fresh lime juice

3 tablespoons Absolut Citron vodka

1 tablespoon triple sec

This frozen take on a classic cosmopolitan cocktail combines cranberry juice and fresh lime juice with citrus vodka and triple sec. Because they don't have any additional sugar, they're light and totally fresh.

1. Whisk all ingredients together in a large bowl.
2. Pour into pop molds, leaving ¼ inch at the top. Freeze until slushy, then insert a stick into each. Freeze overnight, until solid.

Try This! For a fun twist, soak dried cranberries or Craisins in triple sec for a few hours to plump them up. Then, after the pops have been in the freezer for an hour or two, mix the cranberries in. (At this point, the pops should still be slushy.) You could also mix in finely chopped, candied orange peel.

Kamikaze Pops

MAKES ABOUT 8–10 POPS

2 cups water

1½ cups sugar

1 large orange, cut into quarters

¾ cup fresh lime juice (from about 6 large limes)

3 tablespoons vodka

1 tablespoon triple sec

The kamikaze is the first drink I ever ordered in a bar, at midnight on my twenty-first birthday. It was a double, and it pretty near knocked me right out. It's still one of my favorite drinks. This frozen version will give you a cool buzz.

1. Put the water and sugar in a medium-sized pot. Squeeze the orange quarters over the pot to release the juice, then drop them into the pot. Bring to a boil, stirring occasionally until the sugar dissolves. Remove the pot from heat. Cover and let the mixture cool to room temperature.
2. Strain the syrup into a large bowl, discarding the solids. Stir in the lime juice, vodka, and triple sec.
3. Pour into pop molds, leaving ¼ inch at the top. Freeze until slushy, then insert a stick into each. Freeze overnight, until solid.

Blackberry Campari Pops

MAKES ABOUT 5 POPS

½ cup sugar

½ cup water

16 ounces fresh, ripe blackberries (12 ounces for the pops + 4 ounces for garnish)

1 tablespoon fresh lemon juice

3 tablespoons Campari

These pops are a fabulous way to enjoy the ripe, summer flavor of fresh blackberries. Fresh lemon juice and a little Campari add just a hint of tartness.

1. Combine the sugar and water together in a small pot. Bring to a boil over high heat, stirring occasionally, until the sugar completely dissolves. Remove from the heat and cool to room temperature.
2. In your blender, purée the sugar syrup with 12 ounces of the blackberries and the lemon juice. (You may need to do this in batches.) Strain into a large bowl, discarding the seeds and solids. Whisk in the Campari.
3. Divide the remaining 4 ounces of blackberries among the pop molds. Fill with the blackberry mixture, leaving ¼ inch at the top. Freeze until slushy, then insert a stick into each. Freeze overnight, until solid.

Chocolate Martini Pudding Pops

MAKES 8–10 POPS

1 (3.9 ounce) package JELL-O instant chocolate pudding

1 cup whole milk

1 cup heavy cream

1 tablespoon Godiva liqueur

3 tablespoons vodka

These are the ultimate guilty pleasure. Take instant pudding, arguably one of the trashiest foods on the planet, and pair it with a super-luxuriant liqueur. Classy? Probably not. A totally decadent, after-midnight treat? Absolutely. For slightly more refined pops, make them with slow-cooked, homemade chocolate pudding. They'll knock your socks off *and* make Bill Cosby proud.

1. Put the chocolate pudding mix into a large bowl. Add the milk, cream, Godiva liqueur, and vodka. Whisk to combine until uniform.
2. Pour into pop molds, leaving ¼ inch at the top. Freeze until slushy, then insert a stick into each. Freeze overnight, until solid.

Chocolate Liqueur Godiva liqueur has an intense chocolate flavor, but it's a little pricey. For a less expensive pop, substitute the same amount of dark crème de cacao.

Mojito Pops with Fresh Mint

MAKES ABOUT 8–10 POPS

2 cups water

1½ cups sugar

1 cup fresh mint leaves, packed

¾ cup fresh lime juice (from about 6 large limes)

¼ cup light rum

These pops have all the minty charm of a classic mojito—on a stick. Serve them after a big homemade Cuban or Mexican feast. They're the perfect way to quench your palate after a hot and spicy meal.

1. Bring the sugar and water to a boil in a medium-sized pot, whisking occasionally until the sugar dissolves. Remove the pot from heat. Toss in the mint and stir to combine. Cover and let the mixture cool to room temperature.
2. Strain the syrup into a large bowl, discarding the mint. Stir in the lime juice and rum. Pour into pop molds, leaving ¼ inch at the top.
3. Freeze until slushy, then insert a stick into each. Freeze overnight, until solid.

Raspberry Bellini Pops

MAKES ABOUT 8–10 POPS

½ pound ripe, fresh peaches, peeled, pitted, and chopped

½ cup sugar

2 teaspoons fresh lemon juice

1 cup prosecco or cava

1 pint fresh raspberries

These pops are a frosty take on the classic Bellini cocktail, served dotted with fresh raspberries. Use the ripest peaches you can find and they'll be bursting with summer freshness and flavor.

1. Put the peaches, sugar, and lemon juice in a medium-sized pot. Stir to combine. Simmer for about 10 minutes, stirring constantly, until the mixture is thick and jammy. Transfer to your blender and purée until smooth.
2. Pour the purée into a large bowl. Add the prosecco or cava. Stir gently to combine.
3. Divide the raspberries up among the pop molds. Pour the peach mixture over the raspberries, leaving ¼ inch at the top. Freeze until slushy, then insert a stick into each. Freeze overnight, until solid.

Bubbly Tip Don't waste fancy champagne on these. There are plenty of inexpensive sparkling wines (like prosecco or cava) that will do just fine.

Blueberry Basil Martini Pops

MAKES ABOUT 8–10 POPS

1 cup sugar

1 cup water

1½ cups fresh basil, loosely packed

4 cups fresh blueberries

2 tablespoons fresh lemon juice

¼ cup vodka

You might be thinking that blueberry and basil seem like an unlikely couple, but you're in for a ridiculously delicious treat. The pops have a deep berry flavor, with a sweet hint of fragrant pepper from basil-infused simple syrup.

1. Combine the sugar and water together in a small pot. Bring to a boil over high heat, stirring occasionally, until the sugar completely dissolves. Add the basil and stir. Remove from the heat, cover, and cool to room temperature to make a basil-infused simple syrup. Strain, discarding the solids.

2. Purée the blueberries, lemon juice, and basil syrup in your blender in batches. Strain into a large bowl, mashing the purée around with a spoon to extract as much liquid as you can. Discard the solids. Whisk in the vodka.

3. Fill the pop molds with the blueberry mixture, leaving ¼ inch at the top. Freeze until slushy, then insert a stick into each. Freeze overnight, until solid.

Caipirinha Pops with Candied Lime

MAKES ABOUT 8–10 POPS

FOR THE CANDIED LIME

1 large whole lime, sliced into paper-thin rounds

½ cup sugar

½ cup water

FOR THE POPS

¾ cup lime juice (from about 6 large limes)

1½ cups sugar

2 cups water

Zest from 6 large limes

¼ cup cachaça

The caipirinha, Brazil's national cocktail, is made with cachaça, a strong sugar cane brandy that can knock you on your rump if you're not careful. This milder, frozen version is studded with sweet, paper-thin rounds of candied lime.

1. Make the candied lime by slicing the lime into thin rounds. Remove and discard any seeds. Bring a small pot of water to a boil. Drop the slices into boiling water and blanch for about 2 minutes to remove any bitterness. Drain in a colander.

2. Bring the sugar and water to a boil in a small pot over high heat, stirring occasionally. Add the blanched lime slices. Simmer for about 15 minutes, until the slices are translucent. Remove the pot from the heat and let the peels cool to room temperature in the syrup.

3. Remove the cooled peels from the syrup with a slotted spoon and set them on a wire rack overnight, until completely dry. Store between layers of waxed paper in the fridge until ready to use. (These can be prepared up to three days ahead of time.)

4. Make the pops by putting the sugar, water, and lime zest in a medium-sized pot and bringing the mixture to a boil, stirring occasionally until the sugar dissolves. Remove the pot from heat. Transfer the mixture to a bowl and let it cool to room temperature. Strain and discard the solids.

5. Stir in the lime juice and cachaça. Pour the mixture into the pop molds, leaving ¼ inch at the top. Freeze until slushy. Using a stick, insert a couple of candied lime pieces into each pop. Once the lime pieces are in place, leave the stick in as the handle. Freeze overnight, until solid.

Spiced Hard Cider Pops

MAKES 8–10 POPS

2 cups fresh, unfiltered apple cider

3 tablespoons sugar

1¼ cups hard apple cider, such as Woodchuck Cider

¼ teaspoon ground allspice

¼ teaspoon ground cinnamon

⅛ teaspoon ground cloves

8–10 whole cinnamon sticks

These pops get a double dose of apple flavor from fresh cider and hard cider. Try using cinnamon sticks instead of regular wooden sticks for a little extra flavor and a fun, fragrant way to serve.

1. Put the unfiltered apple cider and sugar in a medium-sized pot over high heat. Cook, whisking occasionally, until the mixture just starts to bubble at the edges and the sugar is completely dissolved. Remove from heat, transfer to a bowl, and cool to room temperature.

2. Stir in the hard cider and ground allspice, ground cinnamon, and ground cloves. Pour the mixture into the pop molds, leaving ¼ inch at the top. Freeze until slushy. Insert a whole cinnamon stick into each to serve as the handle. Freeze overnight, until solid.

Cider Tip For the best flavor, get fresh, unfiltered cider from a local orchard if you can. For the hard cider, use regular bottled hard cider, or lighter, sparkling cider.

Chai Tea Pops with Orange Curaçao

MAKES 8–10 POPS

2 cups water

3 chai tea bags

¼ cup light brown sugar

1 whole cinnamon stick

1-inch piece of fresh ginger, peeled and sliced thin

¼ cup orange curaçao

1 cup heavy cream

⅛ teaspoon ground cardamom

These pops are sweet and spicy, just like good chai tea. Brew your own tea with chai tea bags—or go all out and infuse the chai mixture yourself.

1. Bring the water to a boil in a pot on the stove. Remove from heat. Add the chai tea bags, brown sugar, cinnamon stick, and fresh ginger. Cover the pot and let the mixture infuse for about 10 minutes. Strain the mixture, discard the solids, and let cool to room temperature.
2. Whisk in the orange curaçao, cream, and ground cardamom. Pour the mixture into the pop molds, leaving ¼ inch at the top. Freeze until slushy. Insert a stick into each. Freeze overnight, until solid.

Homemade Chai Tea
Makes about 2 cups

It's really easy to make your own chai at home. Here's a simple recipe:

2 cups water
2 tablespoons loose black tea
1 cinnamon stick
5 green cardamom pods, cracked
3 black peppercorns
3 whole cloves
1-inch piece fresh ginger, peeled and sliced thin

Bring all ingredients to a boil in a small pot on the stove. Remove from heat. Cover and infuse for 15 minutes. Strain and cool to room temperature before using.

Watermelon Gimlet Pops

MAKES 8–10 POPS

4½ cups fresh seedless watermelon chunks

2 tablespoons sugar

1 tablespoon fresh lime juice

¼ cup gin

Nothing says summer like fresh watermelon. Except maybe frozen watermelon with gin. (Hello, summer on a stick!) These pops are perfect for hot, sultry nights on the back porch, watching fireflies and shooting stars.

1. Combine the watermelon, sugar, lime juice, and gin in the blender. Blend until smooth.
2. Pour the mixture into the pop molds, leaving ¼ inch at the top. Freeze until slushy. Insert a stick into each. Freeze overnight, until solid.

Mimosa Pops

MAKES 8–10 POPS

2¼ cups freshly squeezed orange juice

3 tablespoons sugar

1 cup prosecco

Try making these pops in skinny, fluted pop molds, which look kind of like a champagne glass. They're the perfect treat to serve houseguests on a lazy Sunday morning, right after brunch.

1. Combine the orange juice and sugar in a large bowl. Whisk until the sugar completely dissolves. Stir in the prosecco.
2. Pour the mixture into the pop molds, leaving ¼ inch at the top. Freeze until slushy. Insert a stick into each. Freeze overnight, until solid.

Chocolate Frangelico Gelato with Toasted Hazelnuts
Chapter 4

Cosmo Pops
Chapter 2

Chocolate Stout Ice Cream
Chapter 3

Bananas Foster Ice Cream
Chapter 3

Hot & Spicy Bloody Mary Granita
Chapter 7

Black Raspberry & Chambord Frappe
Chapter 10

Blueberry Basil Martini Pops
Chapter 2

Cognac & Apricot Sorbet
Chapter 8

Cranberry Mulled Wine Sorbet
Chapter 8

Mini Mint Chocolate Chip Sandwiches
Chapter 9

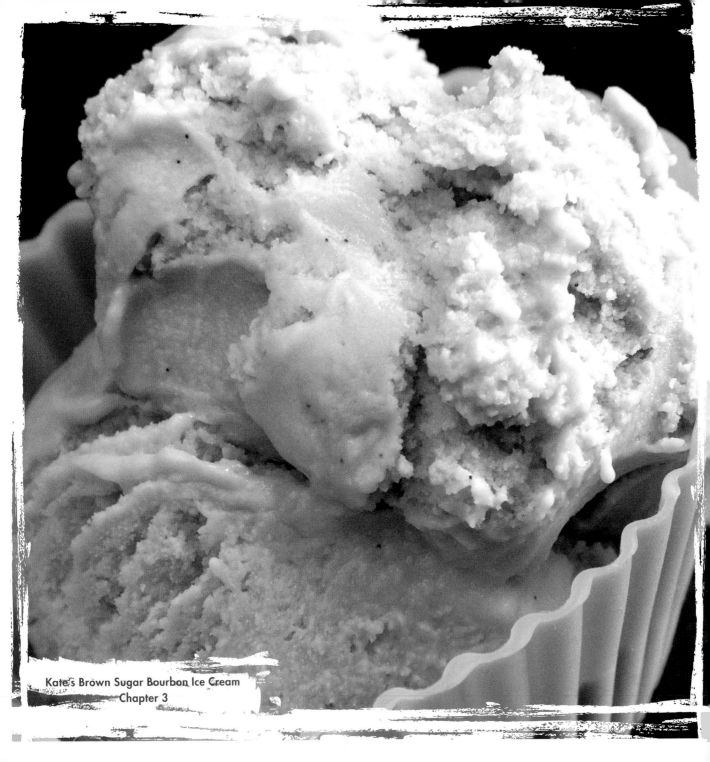

Kate's Brown Sugar Bourbon Ice Cream
Chapter 3

Fiery Chili Lime Tequila Pops
Chapter 2

Frozen Gin Fizz
Chapter 8

Frozen Long Island Iced Tea
Chapter 8

Grand Marnier Frozen Cheesecake
Chapter 9

Strawberry Daiquiri Pops

MAKES 8–10 POPS

4 cups strawberries, hulled and cut into chunks

¾ cup sugar

½ cup water

3 tablespoons fresh lime juice

¼ cup light rum

You won't find anything like these at your local cantina! Ripe, fresh berries give these pops an intense strawberry flavor.

1. Put 3½ cups of the strawberries, sugar, and water in a medium-sized pot. Stir to combine. Simmer for about 5 minutes over medium-high heat, stirring occasionally. Remove from heat and transfer to a bowl. Cool the mixture to room temperature.
2. For more texture, set aside ½ cup of this mixture and then blend the rest until smooth. For less texture, place the entire cooled mixture in the blender and blend until smooth. Transfer to a bowl. Stir in the lime juice, light rum, and remaining ½ cup cut strawberries.
3. Pour the mixture into the pop molds, leaving ¼ inch at the top. Freeze until slushy. Insert a stick into each. Freeze overnight, until solid.

Raspberry Limeade Pops with Chambord

MAKES 8–10 POPS

2 cups water

⅔ cup sugar

Zest of 1 lime

¾ cup fresh lime juice (about 10–12 whole limes)

1 pint fresh raspberries

½ cup Chambord

These pops are a little bit sweet, a little bit tart—and studded with fresh raspberries. They get their slushy, deep red crowns from a drizzle of Chambord in the bottom of the pop mold.

1. Put the water, sugar, lime juice, and lime zest in a medium-sized pot on the stove over high heat. Simmer, whisking occasionally, until the sugar completely dissolves. Remove from heat and cool to room temperature.
2. Drizzle a little Chambord in the bottom of each pop mold. Divide the fresh raspberries up among the molds and drop them in on top of the Chambord. Slowly pour the sugar and lime mixture into the pop molds, leaving ¼ inch at the top. Freeze until slushy. Insert a stick into each. Freeze overnight, until solid.

Chapter 3

Ice Cream

Booze-infused ice cream is pretty darn close to the top of my list of luxurious desserts. Liquor not only contributes a ton of flavor—it also helps keep your ice cream soft and scoopable right out of the freezer. Always choose high-quality ingredients, and use good-quality booze that you would drink.

Ice Cream Making 101

If you've never made ice cream before, never fear. Here's the basic technique.

Mix It Up

Gather your ingredients and equipment and organize your workspace. Whisk the egg yolks and sugar together. Warm the cream and milk together.

Temper the Egg Yolks

Slowly drizzle the warm cream into the egg yolks, whisking constantly. This technique, called *tempering*, raises the temperature of the egg yolks slowly, which keeps them from scrambling. It's what allows you to create the rich, velvety custard base for your ice cream—instead of glop that resembles a failed attempt at making an omelet. This is probably the most difficult part of making ice cream. Once you master it, though, it's a cinch to pull off each time.

Cook the Custard to 170°F

Return the hot egg mixture to the pot and clip a candy thermometer to the inside. Be sure that it doesn't touch the bottom, as that can give you a false reading. Cook over medium heat, whisking constantly. This is important—the whisking helps keep the eggs from congealing on the bottom of the pot. When the mixture hits 170°F, strain it immediately into a large bowl to catch any stray bits of cooked egg.

Chill the Custard in an Ice Bath

Set the bowl in a larger bowl filled with ice, whisking frequently until the custard cools to room temperature. Refrigerate the bowl of custard until it's chilled completely.

Process and Freeze the Ice Cream

Once your mixture is chilled, you're ready to process it in your ice cream maker. Every machine is a little different, so be sure to read the instructions in advance. When it's done, it will probably be about the consistency of soft serve. (Voila, you just made ice cream!)

Remember, if you don't have an ice cream maker, use the method in Chapter 1 to freeze it by hand. Transfer it to a container and freeze overnight. Because of the amount of alcohol in these recipes, they'll need several hours to set up. The hardest part is always the waiting.

Spice Trader's Vanilla Vodka Ice Cream

MAKES ABOUT 1 QUART

6 egg yolks

¾ cup white sugar

2 cups heavy cream

1 cup whole milk

2 whole vanilla beans

1 tablespoon vanilla extract

3 tablespoons vanilla vodka

The key to making really good vanilla ice cream is to start with the best ingredients you can get your paws on. This is a ridiculously rich ice cream that gets its heady fragrance from pure vanilla extract, whole beans, and vanilla vodka. It's thick and creamy and flecked with bits of fresh vanilla bean.

1. Whisk the egg yolks and sugar together in a large bowl. Set aside.
2. Combine the cream and milk in a medium-sized, heavy-bottomed pot. Slit the vanilla bean pods in half lengthwise with a sharp knife. Scrape out the paste with the back of your knife. Add the pods and paste to the pot. Cook the mixture over medium heat, whisking occasionally, until the mixture just starts to bubble at the edges.
3. Remove the pot from the heat. Cover and let the mixture infuse for 15–20 minutes. Remove the vanilla pods and discard. Warm the mixture again on the stove until steaming.
4. Slowly drizzle it into the beaten egg mixture, whisking constantly. Return the combined mixture to the pot. Cook over medium heat, whisking constantly, until it registers 170°F on a candy thermometer and is thick enough to coat the back of a spoon.
5. Remove the pot from the heat. Strain into a large bowl. Whisk in the vanilla extract and vanilla vodka. Cool in an ice bath, whisking frequently to lower the mixture's temperature. Refrigerate until completely chilled, about 4–6 hours.
6. Process the mixture in your ice cream maker according to the manufacturer's instructions. Transfer to a container and freeze overnight.

> *To the Dairy!* If you can, get your cream and eggs from a local dairy. This is a good rule of thumb for all ice cream, but it's a particularly good tip for vanilla, where the milk and cream are paramount to the flavor.

Death by Double Chocolate Liqueur Ice Cream

MAKES ABOUT 1 QUART

6 egg yolks

¾ cup sugar

2 cups heavy cream

1 cup whole milk

5 ounces bittersweet chocolate, chopped

1 tablespoon vanilla extract

3 tablespoons chocolate liqueur

Get ready for chocolate overload! This ice cream is rich and creamy, with a boozy double dose of chocolate flavor from chocolate liqueur and chopped, bittersweet chocolate. Use the highest-quality chocolate you can.

1. In a medium-sized bowl, whisk the egg yolks and sugar together. Set aside.
2. Combine the cream and milk in a medium-sized, heavy-bottomed pot. Cook the mixture over medium heat, whisking occasionally, until the mixture just starts to bubble at the edges. Remove from the heat. Toss in the chopped chocolate. Stir until the chocolate has melted and the mixture is uniform.
3. Slowly, drizzle the hot chocolate mixture into the egg yolks, whisking constantly to combine. Transfer the hot mixture back to your pot.
4. Cook over medium heat, whisking constantly, until it registers 170°F on a candy thermometer and is thick enough to coat the back of a spoon. Strain the mixture into a bowl. Stir in the vanilla extract and chocolate liqueur.
5. Cool in an ice bath, whisking frequently to lower the mixture's temperature. Refrigerate until completely chilled, about 4–6 hours.
6. Process the mixture in your ice cream maker according to the manufacturer's instructions. Transfer to a container and freeze overnight.

Strawberry Daiquiri Ice Cream

MAKES ABOUT 1½ QUARTS

1 pound strawberries, trimmed and sliced

¾ cup white sugar

¼ cup light rum

2¼ cups heavy cream

Zest of 1 large lemon

This ice cream tastes exactly like strawberry whipped cream spiked with rum. And essentially, that's exactly what it is. Serve garnished with whipped cream and fresh sliced strawberries.

1. Nip the stems off of the berries, cut them in half, and put them in a medium-sized bowl with the sugar.
2. Let the mixture sit on the counter for about 15 minutes so the berries start to let out their juice and make a heavenly syrup with the sugar.
3. Working in batches, purée the strawberries and syrup, rum, cream, and lemon zest. Chill until cold.
4. Pour the mixture into your ice cream maker. Process according to the manufacturer's instructions. Transfer to a container and freeze overnight.

Drunken Sailor Ice Cream with Spiced Rum & Candied Orange Peel

MAKES ABOUT 1 QUART

6 egg yolks

¾ cup white sugar

2 cups heavy cream

1 cup whole milk

1 whole vanilla bean

¼ cup spiced rum (like Kraken or Sailor Jerry)

¼ teaspoon ground cinnamon

¼ teaspoon ground cloves

¼ cup candied orange peel, finely chopped

Ahoy! This ice cream would do any old salt proud. With a rich vanilla base, it's fragrant with warm spices and dotted with bits of candied orange peel.

1. Whisk the egg yolks and sugar together in a large bowl. Set aside.
2. Combine the cream and milk in a medium-sized, heavy-bottomed pot. Slit the vanilla bean pod in half lengthwise with a sharp knife. Scrape out the paste with the back of your knife. Add the vanilla pod and paste to the pot. Cook the mixture over medium heat, whisking occasionally, until the mixture just starts to bubble at the edges.
3. Remove the pot from the heat. Cover and let the mixture infuse for 15–20 minutes. Remove the vanilla pod and discard. Warm the mixture again on the stove until steaming.
4. Slowly drizzle it into the beaten egg mixture, whisking constantly. Return the combined mixture to the pot. Cook over medium heat, whisking constantly, until it registers 170°F on a candy thermometer and is thick enough to coat the back of a spoon.
5. Remove the pot from the heat. Strain into a large bowl. Whisk in the spiced rum, ground cinnamon, and ground cloves. Cool in an ice bath, whisking frequently to lower the mixture's temperature. Refrigerate until completely chilled, about 4–6 hours.
6. Process the mixture in your ice cream maker according to the manufacturer's instructions, adding the candied orange peel in the last 5 minutes. Transfer to a container and freeze overnight.

Chocolate Stout Ice Cream

MAKES ABOUT 1 QUART

2 cups heavy cream

½ cup unsweetened cocoa powder

½ cup semisweet chocolate chips

5 egg yolks

¾ cup sugar

½ teaspoon kosher salt

1½ cups chocolate stout

3 tablespoons chocolate liqueur

Chocolate stout is wonderful because it lends itself so easily to cooking and baking. It's fantastic in this ice cream, adding deep, chocolaty flavor. Toss in a little unsweetened cocoa powder and chocolate liqueur for good measure, and it'll be one of the best chocolate ice creams you've had in years!

1. Heat the cream in a medium-sized, heavy-bottomed pot until the mixture just starts to simmer. Remove from the heat and whisk in the cocoa powder and chocolate chips. Set the chocolate cream mixture aside.
2. Put the egg yolks, sugar, and salt in a large bowl. Whisk until smooth.
3. Slowly, drizzle the hot chocolate cream mixture into the egg yolks, whisking constantly to combine. (Do this slowly to temper the eggs, or you'll wind up with scrambled eggs.) When you've added all the chocolate cream, transfer the mixture back to your pot.
4. Cook over medium heat, whisking constantly, until it registers 170°F on a candy thermometer and is thick enough to coat the back of a spoon.
5. Strain the mixture into a large bowl to get rid of any tiny bits of cooked egg. Stir in the chocolate stout and chocolate liqueur. Cool in an ice bath, whisking frequently to lower the mixture's temperature. Refrigerate until completely chilled, about 4–6 hours.
6. Make the ice cream by processing the mixture in your ice cream maker according to the manufacturer's instructions. Transfer to a container and freeze overnight.

Chocolate Overload For over-the-top chocolate madness, add a half cup of miniature chocolate chips during the last 5 minutes in the ice cream maker. Serve in a chocolate cone or a chocolate-dipped waffle cone.

Brandied Eggnog Ice Cream

MAKES ABOUT 1 QUART

6 egg yolks

¾ cup white sugar

2 cups heavy cream

1 cup whole milk

1½ teaspoons freshly grated nutmeg

¼ teaspoon ground cinnamon

3 tablespoons brandy

1 tablespoon vanilla extract

Spiked eggnog is a fixture at most holiday parties. This frosty version is rich with traditional eggnog spices—and a good dose of brandy for a little extra holiday cheer all year round.

1. Whisk the egg yolks and sugar together in a large bowl. Set aside.
2. Put the cream and milk in a medium-sized, heavy-bottomed pot. Cook over medium heat, whisking occasionally, until the mixture just starts to simmer around the edges.
3. Remove the pot from the heat. Slowly drizzle the hot mixture into the egg yolk mixture, whisking constantly to temper it. Return the combined mixture to the pot. Cook over medium heat, whisking constantly, until it registers 170°F on a candy thermometer and is thick enough to coat the back of a spoon.
4. Remove from the heat. Strain the mixture into a large bowl. Stir in the grated nutmeg, ground cinnamon, brandy, and vanilla extract. Cool in an ice bath, whisking frequently to lower the mixture's temperature. Refrigerate until completely chilled, about 4–6 hours.
5. Process in your ice cream maker according to the manufacturer's instructions. Transfer to a container and freeze overnight until solid.

Tipsy Barista

MAKES ABOUT 1½ QUARTS

2 cups heavy cream

½ cup whole milk

¾ cup white sugar

1 cup brewed French Roast coffee, chilled

¼ cup Kahlua

This ice cream tastes just like a big bowl of café au lait spiked with Kahlua. It's definitely sweet, so if you like more of a bitter coffee flavor, cut the sugar down to ½ cup.

1. Whisk all the ingredients together in a large bowl until the sugar has completely dissolved. Refrigerate for about an hour, or until completely chilled.
2. Process in your ice cream maker according to the manufacturer's instructions. Transfer to a container and freeze overnight.

In Case of Ice Cream Emergency If you just have to make this ice cream immediately, here's a trick for chilling freshly brewed coffee quickly. Pour it into a 9" × 13" baking dish. Let it cool to room temperature. Then pop it in the freezer for 10–15 minutes to chill completely.

Candied Bacon Ice Cream with Maple, Whiskey, & Cloves

MAKES ABOUT 1½ QUARTS

CANDIED BACON

4–6 tablespoons granulated maple sugar

6 strips thick-cut bacon

ICE CREAM

6 egg yolks

¾ cup dark brown sugar, packed

2 cups heavy cream

1 cup whole milk

¼ teaspoon ground cloves

¼ cup whiskey or Macallan Amber

½ teaspoon maple extract

6 strips candied bacon, finely chopped

Yep, bacon is everywhere these days—including in this ice cream. Something about the maple-bacon-clove combination is irresistible. This ice cream is warm and spicy—and studded with maple sugar–candied bacon. To add a stronger flavor profile, garnish with a little flaked grey sea salt.

1. Make the candied bacon by preheating your oven to 400°F. Line a sheet pan with foil and set a wire rack on it. Space the bacon out on the rack. Sprinkle each slice with a little granulated maple sugar. Bake until crisp and glossy, 10–15 minutes. Remove the pan from the oven. Flip the bacon over. Sprinkle with more maple sugar. Bake for another 5–10 minutes, until crisp and glossy. Remove the pan from the oven. Let the bacon cool on the rack. Finely chop when cool.

2. Whisk the egg yolks and brown sugar together in a large bowl until uniform. Set aside.

3. Whisk the cream and milk in a medium-sized, heavy-bottomed pot. Cook, whisking occasionally, over medium heat until the mixture just starts to bubble around the edges.

4. Slowly, drizzle the hot mixture into the egg yolk mixture, whisking constantly. Return the mixture to the pot. Cook over medium heat, whisking constantly, until it registers 170°F on a candy thermometer and is thick enough to coat the back of a spoon.

5. Strain the mixture into a large bowl. Stir in the ground cloves, whiskey, and maple extract. Cool in an ice bath, whisking frequently to lower the mixture's temperature. Refrigerate until completely chilled, about 4–6 hours.

6. Process the mixture in your ice cream maker according to the manufacturer's instructions. Add the chopped, candied bacon in the last 5 minutes. Transfer to a container and freeze overnight.

> *Make Ahead* Make the candied bacon a few hours ahead of time so it has plenty of time to cool. If you're a bacon lover, make a double batch. (Just don't blame me if you eat it all beforehand. It's so good.)

Thundering Viking Ice Cream with Spiced Mead

MAKES ABOUT 1 QUART

6 egg yolks

2 cups heavy cream

1 cup whole milk

⅛ teaspoon ground coriander

⅛ teaspoon ground cloves

2 whole vanilla beans

¾ cup honey

½ cup Viking Blood spiced mead

This honey ice cream is laced with spiced mead, a fermented honey wine that's flavored with a variety of spices. Find mead at any well-stocked liquor store, most likely in between the beer and wine. A little ground coriander and cloves bring out the flavor of the mead.

1. Whisk the egg yolks in a large bowl. Set aside.
2. Combine the cream, milk, ground coriander, and ground cloves in a medium-sized, heavy-bottomed pot. Slit the vanilla pods in half lengthwise with a sharp knife. Scrape out the paste with the back of your knife. Add the vanilla pods and paste to the pot. Cook the mixture over medium heat, whisking occasionally, until the mixture just starts to bubble at the edges.
3. Remove the pot from the heat. Cover and let the mixture infuse for 15–20 minutes. Remove the vanilla pods and discard. Warm the mixture again on the stove until steaming.
4. Slowly drizzle it into the beaten egg mixture, whisking constantly. Return the combined mixture to the pot. Cook over medium heat, whisking constantly, until it registers 170°F on a candy thermometer and is thick enough to coat the back of a spoon.
5. Remove the pot from the heat. Strain into a large bowl. Add the honey and spiced mead, whisking until the honey breaks up and the mixture is uniform. Cool in an ice bath, whisking frequently to lower the mixture's temperature. Refrigerate until completely chilled, about 4–6 hours.
6. Process the mixture in your ice cream maker according to the manufacturer's instructions. Transfer to a container and freeze overnight.

Pernod Ice Cream with Australian Licorice

MAKES ABOUT 1 QUART

6 egg yolks

¾ cup white sugar

2 cups heavy cream

1 cup whole milk

25 pieces Australian licorice, finely chopped

¼ cup Pernod

Like black licorice? You're going to love this ice cream. It's flavored with Pernod—and a few handfuls of Australian licorice, a softer type of licorice that's ever so slightly salty. The contrast of flavors and textures makes for an amazing ice cream.

1. Whisk the egg yolks and sugar together in a large bowl. Set aside. Combine the cream, milk, and half the chopped licorice in a medium-sized, heavy-bottomed pot. Reserve the other half of the licorice. Cook the mixture over medium heat, whisking occasionally, until the mixture just starts to bubble at the edges. Purée in the pot using an immersion blender. (If you don't have an immersion blender, purée in batches carefully in your traditional blender.)

2. Remove the pot from the heat. Slowly drizzle the hot mixture into the beaten egg mixture, whisking constantly. Return the combined mixture to the pot. Cook over medium heat, whisking constantly, until it registers 170°F on a candy thermometer and is thick enough to coat the back of a spoon.

3. Remove the pot from the heat. Strain into a large bowl, discarding any chunks of licorice that did not dissolve. Whisk in the Pernod. Cool in an ice bath, whisking frequently to lower the mixture's temperature. Refrigerate until completely chilled, about 4–6 hours.

4. Process the mixture in your ice cream maker according to the manufacturer's instructions, adding in the reserved chopped licorice in the last 5 minutes. Transfer to a container and freeze overnight.

Chop, Chop, Chop Be sure to chop the licorice as small as you can. If the chunks are too large, they won't melt well. Also, you don't want large pieces in the finished ice cream—they'll get rock solid when frozen.

Licorice-Flavored Liquors If you don't have Pernod, try substituting Greek ouzo, Italian sambuca or anisette, or French pastis. If the liquor you choose is sweet, cut the amount of sugar in this recipe down to ½ cup.

Kate's Brown Sugar Bourbon Ice Cream

MAKES ABOUT 1 QUART

6 egg yolks

¾ cup dark brown sugar

2 cups heavy cream

1 cup whole milk

1 vanilla bean

¼ cup bourbon

This sumptuous dessert gets its name from my friend Kate, who said she tried bourbon ice cream a year ago and is still thinking about it. Ice cream that memorable needs to be re-created. This version has lingering notes of bourbon, and it gets a subtle, caramel-tinged sweetness from dark brown sugar.

1. Whisk the egg yolks and brown sugar together in a large bowl. Set aside.
2. Combine the cream and milk in a medium-sized, heavy-bottomed pot. Slit the vanilla pod in half lengthwise with a sharp knife. Scrape out the paste with the back of your knife. Add the vanilla pod and paste to the pot. Cook the mixture over medium heat, whisking occasionally, until the mixture just starts to bubble at the edges.
3. Remove the pot from the heat. Cover and let the mixture infuse for 15–20 minutes. Remove the vanilla pod and discard. Warm the mixture again on the stove until steaming.
4. Slowly drizzle it into the beaten egg mixture, whisking constantly. Return the combined mixture to the pot. Cook over medium heat, whisking constantly, until it registers 170°F on a candy thermometer and is thick enough to coat the back of a spoon.
5. Remove the pot from the heat. Strain into a large bowl. Whisk in the bourbon. Cool in an ice bath, whisking frequently to lower the mixture's temperature. Refrigerate until completely chilled, about 4–6 hours.
6. Process the mixture in your ice cream maker according to the manufacturer's instructions. Transfer to a container and freeze overnight.

> *Something to Remember* All bourbon is whiskey. Not all whiskey is bourbon. Be sure to use a top-shelf liquor, like Maker's Mark, for this recipe to get the sweet smokiness that makes this ice cream so special.

Bananas Foster Ice Cream

MAKES ABOUT 1½ QUARTS

3 tablespoons butter, cut into chunks

3 tablespoons light brown sugar

1½ pounds bananas, peeled and sliced (about 3 medium-sized)

½ cup white sugar

2 cups heavy cream

¼ cup dark rum

This ice cream tastes just like the Bananas Foster you might get at Brennan's, New Orleans's legendary culinary haunt. It blends buttery, caramelized bananas with rich heavy cream and dark rum. And because you don't actually flambé the bananas, the ice cream still has plenty of boozy kick.

1. Melt the butter in a large, nonstick skillet over medium heat. Toss in the brown sugar and sliced bananas. Stir to combine. Cook over medium heat, stirring frequently, until the bananas are light brown and soft, and the sugar and butter have combined into a heavenly, banana-laced caramel sauce.
2. Transfer the hot bananas and sauce into your blender. Purée until smooth.
3. Add the white sugar, cream, and dark rum. Blend until smooth. Chill the mixture for 2–4 hours, or until cold.
4. Pour the mixture into your ice cream maker. Process according to the manufacturer's instructions.
5. Transfer to a container. Freeze overnight and enjoy!

Roasted Bananas If you don't have room on the stove, roast the bananas instead. It takes longer, but the results are just as good. Preheat your oven to 375°F. Put the bananas in a 9" × 13" glass baking dish. Toss with dark brown sugar and chunks of butter. Roast for 25–30 minutes, stirring occasionally, until caramelized.

Mango Sunrise Ice Cream

MAKES ABOUT 1 QUART

1½ cups mango nectar

½ cup sugar

2 cups heavy cream

3 tablespoons tequila

1 tablespoon triple sec

Zest of 1 large orange

Zest of ½ large lemon

2 tablespoons grenadine

Lush, fruity mango nectar provides tons of tropical flavor in this twist on a Tequila Sunrise cocktail. For a little extra work, make this with fresh, puréed mango and increase the amount of sugar to ¾ cup.

1. Put the mango nectar, sugar, and cream in the blender. Blend just until smooth. (Don't overblend, or you'll wind up with whipped cream.) Transfer to a bowl. Stir in the tequila, triple sec, orange zest, and lemon zest. Chill the mixture for 2–4 hours, or until cold.
2. When your mixture is cold, pour it into your ice cream maker. Process according to the manufacturer's instructions. Transfer to a container.
3. Pour the grenadine over the surface. Gently fold it in a couple of times. Don't overdo it. You want to make luscious red swirls—not turn the ice cream pink. Freeze overnight.

Boozy Brazilian Chocolate Truffle Ice Cream

MAKES ABOUT 1½ QUARTS

2 cups heavy cream

2 teaspoons vanilla extract

¼ cup cocoa powder

¼ cup dark crème de cacao

28 ounces sweetened condensed milk

This is a frozen, boozy version of the brigadeiro, a truffle-like Brazilian candy made with sweetened condensed milk, butter, and cocoa powder. It's rich and intensely chocolaty—with just a hint of caramel from the condensed milk. This seriously addictive treat is laced with crème de cacao and tastes just like a frozen chocolate truffle.

1. Put the cream, vanilla extract, and cocoa powder in the bowl of your stand mixer. Beat until they hold soft peaks.
2. Whisk the crème de cacao into the condensed milk. Drizzle it into the cream mixture with the mixer running. Beat until the mixture holds firm peaks.
3. Transfer to a container and freeze overnight.

Condensed Milk vs. Evaporated Milk What's the difference? In a word: sugar. And it's a huge difference. Condensed milk is whole milk that's been slow cooked with sugar until it's reduced by a little more than half. The result is thick, syrupy, and caramel flavored. Evaporated milk is thin and unsweetened. Make sure you walk out of the market with the right can. They're definitely not interchangeable.

Coconut Cream Pie Ice Cream

MAKES 1 QUART

2 cups heavy cream

1 cup coconut milk

¾ cup sugar

¼ cup Malibu rum

1 cup shredded, unsweetened coconut

Depending on where you go in the country, coconut cream pie isn't just a staple in the diner dessert case. It has an inspired following that puts barbecue competitions and blue-ribbon bakeoffs to shame. What we have here is a dense ice cream—laden with coconut milk—that gets beefed up with a couple shots of coconut rum. Shredded coconut provides a little extra texture. Drizzle it with hot fudge sauce for a totally decadent treat.

1. Whisk the cream, coconut milk, sugar, and rum together in a large bowl until the sugar has completely dissolved. Refrigerate until completely chilled.
2. Process in your ice cream maker according to the manufacturer's instructions, adding in the shredded coconut in the last 5 minutes. Transfer to a container and freeze overnight.

Shredded Coconut Shredded coconut comes both sweetened and unsweetened. This recipe uses unsweetened to keep it from being overpoweringly sweet. If you can only find sweetened coconut, use it, but cut the sugar down to ½ cup.

Cherry Bomb Ice Cream

MAKES ABOUT 1 QUART

6 egg yolks

¾ cup sugar

2 cups heavy cream

1 whole vanilla bean

1 cup unsweetened cherry juice

3 tablespoons kirsch or maraschino liqueur

1 tablespoon triple sec

1 cup fresh cherries, stemmed, pitted, and finely chopped

Who doesn't love a nice cherry pie? This ice cream captures that old-school diner flavor. Find bottled cherry juice at a natural food store—or with the fresh juices in the produce section of your grocery store. To make your own, stem and pit about one pound of fresh cherries, then blend and strain. Serve garnished with shortbread cookies or ladyfingers to round out the pie experience.

1. Whisk the egg yolks and sugar together in a large bowl. Set aside.
2. Put the cream in a medium-sized, heavy-bottomed pot. Slit the vanilla bean in half lengthwise with a sharp knife. Scrape out the paste with the back of your knife. Add the vanilla pod and paste to the pot. Cook the mixture over medium heat, whisking occasionally, until the mixture just starts to bubble at the edges.
3. Remove the pot from the heat. Cover and let the mixture infuse for 15–20 minutes. Remove the vanilla pod and discard. Warm the mixture again on the stove until steaming.
4. Slowly drizzle it into the beaten egg mixture, whisking constantly. Return the combined mixture to the pot. Cook over medium heat, whisking constantly, until it registers 170°F on a candy thermometer and is thick enough to coat the back of a spoon.
5. Remove the pot from the heat. Strain into a large bowl. Whisk in the cherry juice, kirsch, and triple sec. Cool in an ice bath, whisking frequently to lower the mixture's temperature. Refrigerate until completely chilled, about 4–6 hours.
6. When your mixture is cold, pour it into your ice cream maker. Process according to the manufacturer's instructions, adding the chopped cherries in the last 5 minutes. Transfer to a container. Freeze overnight.

Chambord Truffle Ice Cream

MAKES ABOUT 1½ QUARTS

6 egg yolks

¾ cup sugar

3 cups fresh raspberries

¼ cup Chambord

¼ cup raspberry jam

2 cups heavy cream

1 cup whole milk

1½ cups dark chocolate chunks

Mmmm, chocolate and raspberry: a match made in heaven. This red raspberry ice cream gets its flavor from fresh berries, raspberry jam, and Chambord—and a ridiculously generous amount of dark chocolate chunks.

1. Whisk the egg yolks and sugar together in a large bowl. Set aside.
2. Put the raspberries, Chambord, and raspberry jam in the blender. Blend until uniform. Strain into a bowl. Set aside.
3. Put the cream and milk in a medium-sized, heavy-bottomed pot. Cook the mixture over medium heat, whisking occasionally, until the mixture just starts to bubble at the edges.
4. Remove the pot from the heat. Slowly drizzle the hot mixture into the beaten egg mixture, whisking constantly. Return the combined mixture to the pot. Cook over medium heat, whisking constantly, until it registers 170°F on a candy thermometer and is thick enough to coat the back of a spoon.
5. Remove the pot from the heat. Strain into a large bowl. Whisk in the strained raspberry Chambord purée. Cool in an ice bath, whisking frequently to lower the mixture's temperature. Refrigerate until completely chilled, about 4–6 hours.
6. When your mixture is cold, pour it into your ice cream maker. Process according to the manufacturer's instructions, adding the chocolate chunks in the last 5 minutes. Transfer to a container. Freeze overnight.

Roasted Peach Daiquiri Ice Cream

MAKES ABOUT 1½ QUARTS

4 ripe peaches, peeled, pitted, and sliced

¼ cup dark brown sugar

4 tablespoons butter

6 egg yolks

¾ cup dark brown sugar

2 cups heavy cream

1 cup peach nectar

¼ cup light rum

Slow roasting the ripe, juicy peaches with butter and brown sugar gives this ice cream a deep, caramelized flavor.

1. Preheat your oven to 400°F. Put the sliced peaches in a 9" × 13" glass baking dish. Toss with dark brown sugar and dot with bits of butter. Roast for about 20 minutes, stirring occasionally.
2. They're done when the peaches are soft enough to mash flat with a fork and the butter and sugar have combined into a delicious caramel sauce. Remove from the oven. Transfer the peaches and sauce into a bowl. Cool to room temperature. Set aside while you make the ice cream.
3. Whisk the egg yolks and sugar in a large bowl. Set aside.
4. Combine the cream and peach nectar in a medium-sized, heavy-bottomed pot. Cook over medium heat, stirring occasionally, until the edges just start to bubble. Remove the pot from the heat.
5. Slowly, drizzle the hot mixture into the egg yolk mixture, whisking constantly. Return the mixture to the pot. Cook over medium heat, whisking constantly, until it registers 170°F on a candy thermometer and is thick enough to coat the back of a spoon.
6. Strain the mixture into a large bowl. Stir in the rum and caramelized peach mixture. Cool in an ice bath, whisking frequently to lower the mixture's temperature. Refrigerate until completely chilled, about 4–6 hours.
7. Process the mixture in your ice cream maker according to the manufacturer's instructions. Transfer to a container and freeze overnight.

Cider Ice Cream with Applejack

MAKES ABOUT 1 QUART

6 egg yolks

1½ cups unfiltered apple cider

¾ cup light brown sugar

2 cups heavy cream

1 cup whole milk

½ teaspoon ground cinnamon

⅛ teaspoon ground cloves

¼ cup applejack

Here in New England, we can't wait for apple-picking season every fall. Aside from baskets of crisp, rosy red apples, it means fresh cider—and lots of it. Reduced apple cider, cinnamon, and ground cloves give this ice cream that fresh-from-the-orchard taste.

1. Whisk the egg yolks together in a large bowl. Set aside.
2. Put the apple cider in a small pot with the brown sugar. Whisk to combine. Simmer to reduce by about half. When the cider is thick and syrupy, take it off the heat.
3. Combine the cream and milk in a medium-sized, heavy-bottomed pot. Cook the mixture over medium heat, whisking occasionally, until the mixture just starts to bubble at the edges. Whisk in the apple cider syrup.
4. Remove the pot from the heat. Slowly drizzle the hot mixture into the beaten egg mixture, whisking constantly. Return the combined mixture to the pot. Cook over medium heat, whisking constantly, until it registers 170°F on a candy thermometer and is thick enough to coat the back of a spoon.
5. Remove the pot from the heat. Strain into a large bowl. Whisk in the ground cinnamon, ground cloves, and applejack. Cool in an ice bath, whisking frequently to lower the mixture's temperature. Refrigerate until completely chilled, about 4–6 hours.
6. Process the mixture in your ice cream maker according to the manufacturer's instructions. Transfer to a container and freeze overnight.

Old-Fashioned Rum Raisin

MAKES ABOUT 1 QUART

1½ cups dark raisins

¾ cup dark rum

6 egg yolks

¾ cup dark brown sugar

2 cups heavy cream

1 cup whole milk

Zest from ½ a large orange

½ teaspoon ground cinnamon

No ice cream section would be complete without a recipe for Rum Raisin. This brown sugar ice cream is studded with rum-soaked raisins—and lightly spiced with cinnamon and fresh orange zest.

1. The day before you're going to make your ice cream, put the raisins and dark rum in a small bowl. Cover and leave on the counter to plump up overnight.
2. Drain the raisins, reserving both the rum and raisins separately.
3. Whisk the egg yolks and brown sugar together in a large bowl. Set aside.
4. Combine the cream, milk, and orange zest in a medium-sized, heavy-bottomed pot. Cook the mixture over medium heat, whisking occasionally, until the mixture just starts to bubble at the edges.
5. Remove the pot from the heat. Slowly drizzle the hot mixture into the beaten egg mixture, whisking constantly. Return the combined mixture to the pot. Cook over medium heat, whisking constantly, until it registers 170°F on a candy thermometer and is thick enough to coat the back of a spoon.
6. Remove the pot from the heat. Strain into a large bowl. Whisk in the ground cinnamon and ¼ cup of the reserved rum from the raisins. (Save the rest of the rum for a Quick Dark & Stormy Cocktail.) Cool in an ice bath, whisking frequently to lower the mixture's temperature. Refrigerate until completely chilled, about 4–6 hours.
7. Process the mixture in your ice cream maker according to the manufacturer's instructions, adding the plumped raisins in the last 5 minutes. Transfer to a container and freeze overnight.

Quick Dark & Stormy Cocktail It would be a crime to let any leftover rum go to waste. (And nothing wrong with a cocktail while you're waiting for your ice cream to churn.)

Toss the leftover rum from the raisins in a glass filled with ice. Top with ginger beer and garnish with a slice of candied ginger.

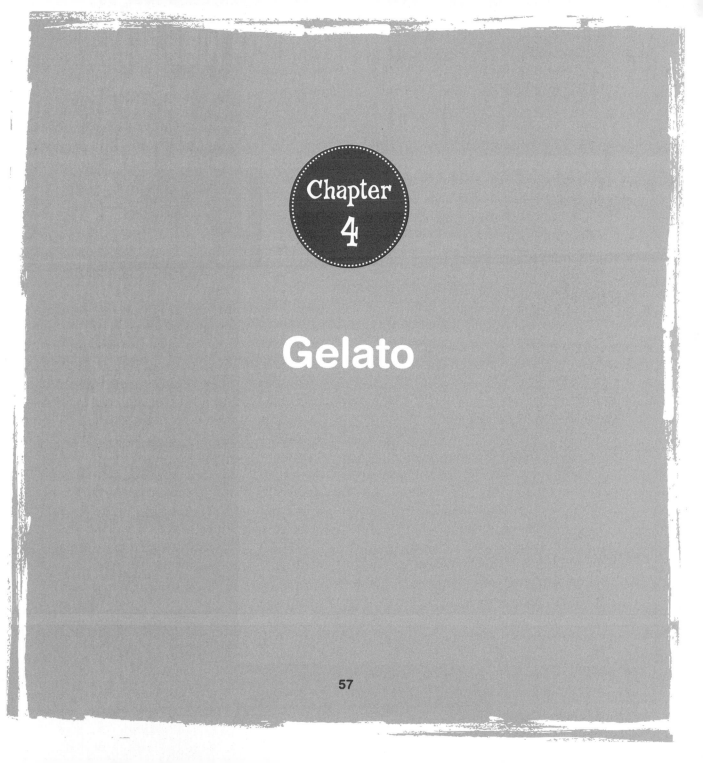

Chapter 4

Gelato

What's the difference between ice cream and gelato? Fat, mainly.

While ice cream is made with more cream than milk, gelato is just the opposite: It's made with more milk than cream—not to mention fewer egg yolks.

Also, true Italian gelato is made with a different kind of machine—one that doesn't aerate the frozen mixture as much as a traditional ice cream machine—which makes for a denser dessert. Rest assured, you can make perfectly delicious gelato at home in your ice cream maker.

The process for making gelato is much the same as for making ice cream, with different proportions of ingredients. To brush up on the basics, see Ice Cream Making 101 in Chapter 3.

Bourbon Vanilla Gelato

MAKES ABOUT 1 QUART

4 egg yolks

¾ cup sugar

2 cups whole milk

1 cup heavy cream

1 whole vanilla bean

¼ cup bourbon vanilla extract

This vanilla-scented gelato is sweet and simple, getting its flavor from Madagascar bourbon vanilla extract—arguably the queen of vanillas. It's the epitome of old-fashioned vanilla flavor. If you don't have bourbon vanilla extract, use the highest-quality extract you can get your hands on—or make your own (see Chapter 11).

1. Whisk the egg yolks and sugar in a large bowl. Set aside.
2. Combine the milk and cream in a medium-sized, heavy-bottomed pot. Slit the vanilla bean in half lengthwise with a sharp knife. Scrape out the paste with the back of your knife. Add the vanilla pod and paste to the pot. Cook the mixture over medium heat, whisking occasionally, until the mixture just starts to bubble at the edges.
3. Remove the pot from the heat. Cover and let the mixture infuse for 15–20 minutes. Remove the vanilla pod and discard. Warm the mixture again on the stove until steaming.
4. Slowly, drizzle the hot mixture into the egg yolk mixture, whisking constantly. Return the mixture to the pot. Cook over medium heat, whisking constantly, until it registers 170°F on a candy thermometer and is thick enough to coat the back of a spoon.
5. Strain the mixture into a large bowl. Stir in the bourbon vanilla extract. Cool in an ice bath, whisking frequently to lower the mixture's temperature. Refrigerate until completely chilled, about 4–6 hours.
6. Process the mixture in your ice cream maker according to the manufacturer's instructions. Transfer to a container and freeze overnight.

Chocolate Frangelico Gelato with Toasted Hazelnuts

MAKES ABOUT 1½ QUARTS

1 cup whole hazelnuts, shelled

4 egg yolks

½ cup sugar

2 cups whole milk

1 cup heavy cream

1 whole vanilla bean

1 cup Nutella

¼ cup Frangelico

If you're like me, and you're guilty of sneaking midnight spoonfuls of Nutella straight out of the jar, you're going to love this gelato. The rich, chocolate hazelnut spread plays a starring role, supported by toasted hazelnuts and nutty Frangelico liqueur.

1. Preheat your oven to 350°F. Spread the hazelnuts out on a sheet pan. Roast for 5–10 minutes, until warm and fragrant. Keep a close eye on them so they don't burn. Remove the pan from the oven and transfer the nuts to a plate to cool. When cool, chop into smallish pieces and set aside.
2. Whisk the egg yolks and sugar together in a large bowl. Set aside.
3. Combine the milk and cream in a medium-sized, heavy-bottomed pot. Split the vanilla bean lengthwise with a sharp knife. Scrape the paste out with the back of the knife. Add the vanilla paste and pod to the pot. Cook over medium heat, whisking constantly to dissolve the sugar, until the mixture just starts to simmer.
4. Remove the pot from the heat. Cover and let the mixture infuse for 15–20 minutes. Remove the vanilla pod and discard. Warm the mixture again on the stove until steaming.
5. Slowly drizzle it into the beaten egg mixture, whisking constantly. Return the mixture to your pot. Cook over medium heat, whisking constantly, until it registers 170°F on a candy thermometer and is thick enough to coat the back of a spoon.
6. Strain the mixture into a large bowl. Whisk in the Nutella and Frangelico. Cool in an ice bath, whisking frequently to lower the mixture's temperature. Refrigerate until completely chilled, about 4–6 hours.
7. Process the mixture in your ice cream maker according to the manufacturer's instructions, adding in the chopped, toasted hazelnuts in the last 5 minutes. Transfer to a container and freeze overnight.

St. Germaine & Earl Grey Tea Gelato

MAKES ABOUT 1 QUART

4 egg yolks

¾ cup sugar

2 cups whole milk

1 cup heavy cream

¼ cup loose Earl Grey tea

⅓ cup St. Germaine elderflower liqueur

This delightful gelato pairs St. Germaine—a sweet, French elderflower liqueur—with Earl Grey tea, an aromatic brew that gets its citrus flavor from bergamot oil.

1. Whisk the egg yolks and sugar in a large bowl. Set aside.
2. Combine the milk, cream, and tea in a medium-sized, heavy-bottomed pot. Cook over medium heat, stirring occasionally, until the edges just start to bubble. Remove the pot from the heat. Cover the pot and let it sit for about 15 minutes to infuse. Strain and discard the solids.
3. Return the pot to the stove, uncovered, and bring it to a simmer over medium-high heat. Remove the pot from the stove. Slowly, drizzle the hot mixture into the egg yolk mixture, whisking constantly. Return the mixture to the pot. Cook over medium heat, whisking constantly, until it registers 170°F on a candy thermometer and is thick enough to coat the back of a spoon.
4. Strain the mixture into a large bowl. Stir in the St. Germaine. Cool in an ice bath, whisking frequently to lower the mixture's temperature. Refrigerate until completely chilled, about 4–6 hours.
5. Process the mixture in your ice cream maker according to the manufacturer's instructions. Transfer to a container and freeze overnight.

Marsala-Spiked Zabaglione Gelato

MAKES ABOUT 1 QUART

4 egg yolks

¾ cup sugar

2 cups whole milk

1 cup heavy cream

1 teaspoon vanilla extract

½ cup Marsala wine

What the heck is a zabaglione? Simple. It's a light Italian custard made with egg yolks, sugar, and Marsala. Here's a scrumptious frozen version.

1. Whisk the egg yolks and sugar in a large bowl. Set aside.
2. Combine the milk and cream in a medium-sized, heavy-bottomed pot. Cook over medium heat, stirring occasionally, until the edges just start to bubble. Remove the pot from the heat.
3. Slowly, drizzle the hot mixture into the egg yolk mixture, whisking constantly. Return the mixture to the pot. Cook over medium heat, whisking constantly, until it registers 170°F on a candy thermometer and is thick enough to coat the back of a spoon.
4. Strain the mixture into a large bowl. Stir in the vanilla extract and Marsala. Cool in an ice bath, whisking frequently to lower the mixture's temperature. Refrigerate until completely chilled, about 4–6 hours.
5. Process the mixture in your ice cream maker according to the manufacturer's instructions. Transfer to a container and freeze overnight.

Get Figgy In Italy, zabaglione is traditionally served with figs. If you can't find fresh figs, serve with a dollop or two of good-quality fig preserves.

White Chocolate Liqueur Gelato

MAKES ABOUT 1 QUART

4 egg yolks

¾ cup sugar

2 cups whole milk

1 cup heavy cream

6 ounces white chocolate, finely chopped

1 teaspoon vanilla extract

¼ cup light crème de cacao

This is a far cry from the waxy white chocolate Easter bunny you got when you were a kid. Because white chocolate is basically cocoa butter, it makes for an incredibly rich, velvety gelato, with just a hint of refined chocolate flavor.

1. Whisk the egg yolks and sugar together in a large bowl. Set aside.
2. Combine the milk and cream in a medium-sized, heavy-bottomed pot. Cook over medium heat, stirring occasionally, until the edges just start to bubble. Remove the pot from the heat.
3. Add the chopped white chocolate to the hot milk mixture. Stir to combine until completely melted.
4. Slowly, drizzle the hot mixture into the egg yolk mixture, whisking constantly. Return the mixture to the pot. Cook over medium heat, whisking constantly, until it registers 170°F on a candy thermometer and is thick enough to coat the back of a spoon.
5. Strain the mixture into a large bowl. Stir in the vanilla extract and light crème de cacao. Cool in an ice bath, whisking frequently to lower the mixture's temperature. Refrigerate until completely chilled, about 4–6 hours.
6. Process the mixture in your ice cream maker according to the manufacturer's instructions. Transfer to a container and freeze overnight.

> *Just What Is White Chocolate, Anyway?* Technically, white chocolate isn't chocolate. Made up of cocoa butter, sugar, and milk solids, it lacks the cocoa solids that give milk and dark chocolate their rich, chocolate flavor and dark color. Use the highest-quality white chocolate you can find for this recipe.

Caramel Apple Brandy Gelato

MAKES ABOUT 1½ QUARTS

3 large Granny Smith apples, peeled, cored, and cut into small chunks

¼ cup light brown sugar

4 tablespoons butter

4 egg yolks

½ cup sugar

2 cups whole milk

1 cup heavy cream

½ teaspoon ground cinnamon

¼ teaspoon ground cardamom

1 teaspoon vanilla extract

¼ cup Calvados

⅔ cup dulce de leche, at room temperature

This recipe captures that autumn, county fair flavor of caramel apples—in a gelato that's a heck of a lot easier to eat. A thick swirl of dulce de leche adds more rich, caramel-y goodness that won't stick to your teeth. This recipe looks more complicated than it is. Basically, you're roasting some apples, adding them to a spiced gelato base, and swirling it with dulce de leche.

1. Preheat your oven to 400°F. Put the apple chunks in a 9" × 13" glass baking dish. Toss with light brown sugar and dot with bits of butter. Roast for 25–30 minutes, stirring occasionally, until the apples are soft enough to mash flat with a fork and the butter and sugar have combined into a delicious caramel sauce.

2. Remove from the oven. Transfer the apples and sauce into a bowl. Cool to room temperature, then refrigerate until completely chilled.

3. Whisk the egg yolks and sugar in a large bowl until light yellow and fluffy. Set aside.

4. Combine the milk, cream, cinnamon, and cardamom in a medium-sized, heavy-bottomed pot. Cook over medium heat, stirring occasionally, until the edges just start to bubble. Remove the pot from the heat.

5. Slowly, drizzle the hot mixture into the egg yolk mixture, whisking constantly. Return the mixture to the pot. Cook over medium heat, whisking constantly, until it registers 170°F on a candy thermometer and is thick enough to coat the back of a spoon.

6. Strain the mixture into a large bowl. Stir in the vanilla extract, apples, sauce, and Calvados. Cool in an ice bath, whisking frequently to lower the mixture's temperature. Refrigerate until completely chilled, about 4–6 hours.

7. Process the mixture in your ice cream maker according to the manufacturer's instructions. Transfer to a container. Drizzle the dulce de leche over the gelato and swirl through with a knife. Freeze overnight.

Kirsch-Infused Slippery Cherry Sherbet
Chapter 8

White Chocolate Liqueur Gelato
Chapter 4

Whiskey & Fig Gelato
Chapter 4

Pumpkin Pie Frozen Yogurt with Spiced Rum
Chapter 5

Homemade Maraschino Cherries
Chapter 11

Molasses & Ginger Brandy Ice Cream Sandwiches
Chapter 9

Smooth Dark & Stormy
Chapter 8

Vietnamese Coffee Gelato
Chapter 4

Peppermint Patty Gelato
Chapter 4

Frozen Kahlua Cheesecake
Chapter 9

Roasted Pear Gelato with Eau de Vie
Chapter 4

Tipsy Witch Granita Infused with Rosemary & Lemon
Chapter 7

Campari & Lemon Gelato
Chapter 4

Toasted Amaretto Gelato
Chapter 4

Roasted Pear Gelato with Eau de Vie

MAKES ABOUT 1 QUART

4 Bosc pears, peeled, seeded, and cut into small chunks

¼ cup light brown sugar

4 tablespoons butter

4 egg yolks

¾ cup light brown sugar

2 cups whole milk

1 cup heavy cream

1 teaspoon vanilla extract

3 tablespoons pear eau de vie

This caramel-tinged gelato gets its deep fruit flavor from roasted pears and pear eau de vie. Don't blame me if your neighbors come sniffing around when you make this. The roasted pears will make your house smell insanely good!

1. Preheat your oven to 400°F. Put the pear chunks in a 9" × 13" glass baking dish. Toss with light brown sugar and dot with bits of butter. Roast for 25–30 minutes, stirring occasionally, until they're soft enough to mash flat with a fork and the butter and sugar have combined into a delicious caramel sauce.
2. Remove from the oven. Transfer the pears and all that luscious sauce into a bowl. Cool to room temperature, then refrigerate until completely chilled.
3. Whisk the egg yolks and sugar in a large bowl. Set aside.
4. Combine the milk and cream in a medium-sized, heavy-bottomed pot. Cook over medium heat, stirring occasionally, until the edges just start to bubble. Remove the pot from the heat.
5. Slowly, drizzle the hot mixture into the egg yolk mixture, whisking constantly. Return the mixture to the pot. Cook over medium heat, whisking constantly, until it registers 170°F on a candy thermometer and is thick enough to coat the back of a spoon.
6. Strain the mixture into a large bowl. Stir in the vanilla extract, pear eau de vie, and chilled caramelized pear mixture. Cool in an ice bath, whisking frequently to lower the mixture's temperature. Refrigerate until completely chilled, about 4–6 hours.
7. Process the mixture in your ice cream maker according to the manufacturer's instructions. Transfer to a container and freeze overnight.

Rumple Minze Gelato

MAKES ABOUT 1 QUART

4 egg yolks

½ cup sugar

2 cups whole milk

1 cup heavy cream

⅛ teaspoon peppermint extract

¼ cup Rumple Minze

¾ cup crushed peppermint hard candies or candy canes

This is a fantastic way to use up all those extra candy canes during the winter holidays. Serve small bowls of this after you go a-caroling, garnished with a miniature candy cane or a piece of white chocolate peppermint bark.

1. Whisk the egg yolks and sugar in a large bowl. Set aside.
2. Combine the milk and cream in a medium-sized, heavy-bottomed pot. Cook over medium heat, stirring occasionally, until the edges just start to bubble. Remove the pot from the heat.
3. Slowly, drizzle the hot mixture into the egg yolk mixture, whisking constantly. Return the mixture to the pot. Cook over medium heat, whisking constantly, until it registers 170°F on a candy thermometer and is thick enough to coat the back of a spoon.
4. Strain the mixture into a large bowl. Stir in the peppermint extract and Rumple Minze. Cool in an ice bath, whisking frequently to lower the mixture's temperature. Refrigerate until completely chilled, about 4–6 hours.
5. Process the mixture in your ice cream maker according to the manufacturer's instructions, adding the crushed candies in during the last 5 minutes. Transfer to a container and freeze overnight.

> *Would You Like Chocolate with That?* Try adding in ½ cup of chopped white chocolate peppermint bark along with the crushed peppermint candies.

Whiskey & Fig Gelato

MAKES ABOUT 1 QUART

4 egg yolks

2 cups whole milk

1 cup heavy cream

¾ cup fig preserves

Zest from ½ large lemon

¼ cup whiskey

½ cup honey

Whiskey, figs, and honey are an outstanding combination. Something about the earthiness of whiskey is the perfect companion to the sweetness of the figs. Use good-quality fig preserves for this gelato. Or, if figs are in season and you're feeling inspired, make your own.

1. Whisk the egg yolks together in a large bowl. Set aside.
2. Combine the milk and cream in a medium-sized, heavy-bottomed pot. Cook over medium heat, stirring occasionally, until the edges just start to bubble. Remove the pot from the heat.
3. Slowly, drizzle the hot mixture into the egg yolks, whisking constantly. Return the mixture to the pot. Cook over medium heat, whisking constantly, until it registers 170°F on a candy thermometer and is thick enough to coat the back of a spoon.
4. Strain the mixture into a large bowl. Whisk in the fig preserves, lemon zest, and whiskey. Then, whisk in the honey bit by bit, tasting as you go, until you're happy with the level of sweetness. Cool in an ice bath, whisking frequently to lower the mixture's temperature. Refrigerate until completely chilled, about 4–6 hours.
5. Process the mixture in your ice cream maker according to the manufacturer's instructions. Transfer to a container and freeze overnight.

Caramel Scotch Gelato

MAKES ABOUT 1 QUART

4 egg yolks

½ cup sugar

2 cups whole milk

1 cup heavy cream

1 teaspoon vanilla extract

¾ cup dulce de leche

¼ cup Scotch

Talk about a manly gelato. Serve to your favorite pack of gentlemen hounds at their next cigar night. For a quick ice cream cocktail, put two large scoops in a rocks glass and top with a shot of good Scotch.

1. Whisk the egg yolks and sugar in a large bowl. Set aside.
2. Combine the milk and cream in a medium-sized, heavy-bottomed pot. Cook over medium heat, stirring occasionally, until the edges just start to bubble. Remove the pot from the heat.
3. Slowly, drizzle the hot mixture into the egg yolk mixture, whisking constantly. Return the mixture to the pot. Cook over medium heat, whisking constantly, until it registers 170°F on a candy thermometer and is thick enough to coat the back of a spoon.
4. Strain the mixture into a large bowl. Add the vanilla extract, dulce de leche, and Scotch, whisking until the dulce de leche has broken up and the mixture is uniform. Cool in an ice bath, whisking frequently to lower the mixture's temperature. Refrigerate until completely chilled, about 4–6 hours.
5. Process the mixture in your ice cream maker according to the manufacturer's instructions. Transfer to a container and freeze overnight.

Toasted Amaretto Gelato

MAKES ABOUT 1 QUART

1 cup sliced almonds

4 egg yolks

¾ cup sugar

¾ cup almond paste, grated

2 cups whole milk

1 cup heavy cream

1 teaspoon vanilla extract

1 teaspoon pure almond extract

¼ cup Amaretto

Between almond paste, almond extract, Amaretto, and toasted almond slices, this gelato is on almond-y overload. The sliced almonds add a little crunch and texture. For a smoother gelato, leave them out. You'll still have plenty of flavor.

1. Preheat your oven to 350°F. Spread the sliced almonds out on a sheet pan. Roast for 5–10 minutes, until warm and fragrant. Keep a close eye on them so they don't burn. Remove the pan from oven and transfer the nuts to a plate to cool.
2. Whisk the egg yolks, sugar, and almond paste in a large bowl. Set aside.
3. Combine the milk and cream in a medium-sized, heavy-bottomed pot. Cook over medium heat, stirring occasionally, until the edges just start to bubble. Remove the pot from the heat.
4. Slowly, drizzle the hot mixture into the egg yolk mixture, whisking constantly. Return the mixture to the pot. Cook over medium heat, whisking constantly, until it registers 170°F on a candy thermometer and is thick enough to coat the back of a spoon.
5. Strain the mixture into a large bowl. Whisk in the vanilla extract, almond extract, and Amaretto. Cool in an ice bath, whisking frequently to lower the mixture's temperature. Refrigerate until completely chilled, about 4–6 hours.
6. Process the mixture in your ice cream maker according to the manufacturer's instructions, adding in the toasted almonds in the last 5 minutes. Transfer to a container and freeze overnight.

Almond Paste vs. Marzipan Both are made with ground almonds and sugar. What's the difference? Straight almond paste will have a higher percentage of almonds, so it's more almond bang for your buck. Marzipan is kind of like ready-made candy, with a lot more sugar. Almond paste is firm, like Play-Doh. Grate it just like a piece of Parmesan.

Strawberry Basil Gelato

MAKES ABOUT 1½ QUARTS

1 cup strawberries, hulled and sliced

4 egg yolks

½ cup sugar, divided

2 cups whole milk

1 cup heavy cream

1 cup fresh basil leaves, loosely packed

1 cup strawberry preserves

¼ cup strawberry liqueur

There's nothing quite like fresh strawberries from your own garden—or a local farmers' market. Fresh basil gives this refreshing gelato a slight peppery bite that enhances the flavor of the berries.

1. Macerate the strawberries by putting them in a bowl and tossing with ¼ cup of sugar. Set aside for about 30 minutes.
2. Whisk the egg yolks and the remaining ¼ cup of sugar in a large bowl. Set aside.
3. Combine the milk and cream in a medium-sized, heavy-bottomed pot. Cook over medium heat, stirring occasionally, until the edges just start to bubble. Remove the pot from the heat. Stir in the fresh basil. Cover and let the mixture infuse for 10 minutes. Strain and discard the basil leaves.
4. Slowly, drizzle the hot mixture into the egg yolk mixture, whisking constantly. Return the mixture to the pot. Cook over medium heat, whisking constantly, until it registers 170°F on a candy thermometer and is thick enough to coat the back of a spoon.
5. Strain the mixture into a large bowl. Whisk in the strawberry preserves, strawberry liqueur, and sliced strawberry mixture with syrup. Cool in an ice bath, whisking frequently to lower the mixture's temperature. Refrigerate until completely chilled, about 4–6 hours.
6. Process the mixture in your ice cream maker according to the manufacturer's instructions. Transfer to a container and freeze overnight.

Raspberry Lambic Gelato

MAKES ABOUT 1 QUART

4 egg yolks

½ cup sugar

2 cups whole milk

1 cup heavy cream

½ cup raspberry lambic

¼ cup raspberry preserves

Raspberry lambic is a Belgian beer that's fermented using raspberries. A heady, bubbly brew that's one part fruit spritzer and one part beer, it makes for a sweet and earthy gelato.

1. Whisk the egg yolks and sugar in a large bowl. Set aside.
2. Combine the milk and cream in a medium-sized, heavy-bottomed pot. Cook over medium heat, stirring occasionally, until the edges just start to bubble. Remove the pot from the heat.
3. Slowly, drizzle the hot mixture into the egg yolk mixture, whisking constantly. Return the mixture to the pot. Cook over medium heat, whisking constantly, until it registers 170°F on a candy thermometer and is thick enough to coat the back of a spoon.
4. Strain the mixture into a large bowl. Whisk in the raspberry lambic and raspberry preserves. Cool in an ice bath, whisking frequently to lower the mixture's temperature. Refrigerate until completely chilled, about 4–6 hours.
5. Process the mixture in your ice cream maker according to the manufacturer's instructions. Transfer to a container and freeze overnight.

Hot & Smoky Peach Schnapps Gelato

MAKES ABOUT 1 QUART

4 egg yolks

½ cup sugar

2 cups whole milk

1 cup heavy cream

¼ teaspoon ground chipotle pepper

¼ cup peach schnapps

¼ cup peach jam

A peach is one of those versatile fruits that's just as comfy in a pie or a cocktail as it is in a spicy salsa. This gelato is sunny and sweet, with a hint of smoky fire from a little ground chipotle. If you like, make the roasted peaches from the Roasted Peach Daiquiri Ice Cream recipe in Chapter 3 and use ¼ cup here in place of the peach jam.

1. Whisk the egg yolks and sugar in a large bowl. Set aside.
2. Combine the milk and cream in a medium-sized, heavy-bottomed pot. Cook over medium heat, stirring occasionally, until the edges just start to bubble. Remove the pot from the heat.
3. Slowly, drizzle the hot mixture into the egg yolk mixture, whisking constantly. Return the mixture to the pot. Cook over medium heat, whisking constantly, until it registers 170°F on a candy thermometer and is thick enough to coat the back of a spoon.
4. Strain the mixture into a large bowl. Whisk in the ground chipotle, peach schnapps, and peach jam. Cool in an ice bath, whisking frequently to lower the mixture's temperature. Refrigerate until completely chilled, about 4–6 hours.
5. Process the mixture in your ice cream maker according to the manufacturer's instructions. Transfer to a container and freeze overnight.

Vietnamese Coffee Gelato

MAKES ABOUT 1 QUART

4 egg yolks

½ cup sugar

2 cups whole milk

1 cup heavy cream

1½ tablespoons instant espresso powder

½ a 14-ounce can of sweetened condensed milk

¼ cup espresso-flavored vodka

Vietnamese iced coffee is made with strong, black coffee liberally laced with sweetened condensed milk. It's strong and sweet—just like this gelato.

1. Whisk the egg yolks and sugar in a large bowl. Set aside.
2. Put the milk, cream, and espresso powder in a medium-sized, heavy-bottomed pot. Cook over medium heat, stirring occasionally, until the edges just start to bubble. Remove the pot from the heat.
3. Slowly, drizzle the hot mixture into the egg yolk mixture, whisking constantly. Return the mixture to the pot. Cook over medium heat, whisking constantly, until it registers 170°F on a candy thermometer and is thick enough to coat the back of a spoon.
4. Strain the mixture into a large bowl. Whisk in the condensed milk and espresso-flavored vodka. Cool in an ice bath, whisking frequently to lower the mixture's temperature. Refrigerate until completely chilled, about 4–6 hours.
5. Process the mixture in your ice cream maker according to the manufacturer's instructions. Transfer to a container and freeze overnight.

Condensed Milk vs. Evaporated Milk What's the difference? In a word: sugar. And it's a huge difference. Condensed milk is whole milk that's been slow cooked with sugar until it's reduced by a little more than half. The result is thick, syrupy, and caramel flavored. Evaporated milk is thin and unsweetened. Make sure you walk out of the market with the right can. They're definitely not interchangeable.

Grasshopper Gelato

MAKES ABOUT 1 QUART

4 egg yolks

½ cup sugar

2 cups whole milk

1 cup heavy cream

⅓ cup green crème de menthe

Mint leaves, for garnish

What's pastel green, refreshingly minty, and won't hop away when you set it down on the bar? This gelato gets that trademark Grasshopper cocktail color from a generous amount of green crème de menthe.

1. Whisk the egg yolks and sugar in a large bowl. Set aside.
2. Put the milk and cream in a medium-sized, heavy-bottomed pot. Cook over medium heat, stirring occasionally, until the edges just start to bubble. Remove the pot from the heat.
3. Slowly, drizzle the hot mixture into the egg yolk mixture, whisking constantly. Return the mixture to the pot. Cook over medium heat, whisking constantly, until it registers 170°F on a candy thermometer and is thick enough to coat the back of a spoon.
4. Strain the mixture into a large bowl. Whisk in the crème de menthe. Cool in an ice bath, whisking frequently to lower the mixture's temperature. Refrigerate until completely chilled, about 4–6 hours.
5. Process the mixture in your ice cream maker according to the manufacturer's instructions. Transfer to a container and freeze overnight.
6. Serve garnished with fresh mint leaves.

> *Mint Chocolate Chip Gelato* This gelato makes a fabulous base for mint chocolate chip gelato—right down to the color. Simply add in ½ –1 cup of mini dark chocolate chips, shaved dark chocolate, or dark chocolate chunks in the last 5 minutes in the ice cream maker.

Peppermint Patty Gelato

MAKES ABOUT 1 QUART

4 egg yolks

½ cup sugar

2 cups whole milk

1 cup heavy cream

⅛ teaspoon peppermint extract

¼ cup peppermint schnapps

1 cup peppermint patties, chopped

Small, whole peppermint patties, for garnish

Get ready: This super minty gelato may just blow you away. For a little more chocolate, toss in ½ cup of mini chocolate chips along with the chopped peppermint patties. For a more subtle mint flavor, substitute light crème de menthe for the peppermint schnapps.

1. Whisk the egg yolks and sugar in a large bowl. Set aside.
2. Put the milk and cream in a medium-sized, heavy-bottomed pot. Cook over medium heat, stirring occasionally, until the edges just start to bubble. Remove the pot from the heat.
3. Slowly, drizzle the hot mixture into the egg yolk mixture, whisking constantly. Return the mixture to the pot. Cook over medium heat, whisking constantly, until it registers 170°F on a candy thermometer and is thick enough to coat the back of a spoon.
4. Strain the mixture into a large bowl. Whisk in the peppermint extract and peppermint schnapps. Cool in an ice bath, whisking frequently to lower the mixture's temperature. Refrigerate until completely chilled, about 4–6 hours.
5. Process the mixture in your ice cream maker according to the manufacturer's instructions, adding in the chopped peppermint patties in the last 5 minutes. Transfer to a container and freeze overnight.
6. Serve garnished with a small peppermint patty.

Campari & Lemon Gelato

MAKES ABOUT 1½ QUARTS

4 egg yolks

¼ cup sugar

2 cups whole milk

1 cup heavy cream

1 cup lemon curd

Zest from ½ large lemon

1 tablespoon Campari

1 tablespoon gin

Bitters are everywhere in the bar scene these days. This gelato gets its herbal flavor from a little gin and a splash of bright red Campari. Creamy, sweet-tart lemon curd and lemon zest give it bright, citrus notes. This recipe errs on the less bitter side. Taste the custard mixture once you whisk in the liquors. For a more pronounced bitters flavor, add a little more Campari. (But be careful, a little goes a long way!)

1. Whisk the egg yolks together in a large bowl. Set aside.
2. Combine the milk and cream in a medium-sized, heavy-bottomed pot. Cook over medium heat, stirring occasionally, until the edges just start to bubble. Remove the pot from the heat.
3. Slowly, drizzle the hot mixture into the egg yolks, whisking constantly. Return the mixture to the pot. Cook over medium heat, whisking constantly, until it registers 170°F on a candy thermometer and is thick enough to coat the back of a spoon.
4. Strain the mixture into a large bowl. Whisk in the lemon curd, lemon zest, Campari, and gin. Cool in an ice bath, whisking frequently to lower the mixture's temperature. Refrigerate until completely chilled, about 4–6 hours.
5. Process the mixture in your ice cream maker according to the manufacturer's instructions. Transfer to a container and freeze overnight.

White Russian Gelato

MAKES ABOUT 1 QUART

4 egg yolks

½ cup sugar

2 cups whole milk

1 cup heavy cream

½ cup Kahlua

Chocolate whipped cream, for garnish

Shaved dark chocolate, for garnish

Like the eponymous cocktail, this smooth, creamy gelato has just a hint of coffee flavor. Serve garnished with chocolate-flavored whipped cream or shaved dark chocolate.

1. Whisk the egg yolks and sugar in a large bowl. Set aside.
2. Put the milk and cream in a medium-sized, heavy-bottomed pot. Cook over medium heat, stirring occasionally, until the edges just start to bubble. Remove the pot from the heat.
3. Slowly, drizzle the hot mixture into the egg yolk mixture, whisking constantly. Return the mixture to the pot. Cook over medium heat, whisking constantly, until it registers 170°F on a candy thermometer and is thick enough to coat the back of a spoon.
4. Strain the mixture into a large bowl. Whisk in the Kahlua. Cool in an ice bath, whisking frequently to lower the mixture's temperature. Refrigerate until completely chilled, about 4–6 hours.
5. Process the mixture in your ice cream maker according to the manufacturer's instructions. Transfer to a container and freeze overnight.
6. Serve garnished with the chocolate whipped cream and shaved dark chocolate.

Chocolate Whipped Cream
You can get chocolate whipped cream in a can at the market, but it's really easy to make your own.

½ cup heavy cream

1 teaspoon unsweetened cocoa powder

1 teaspoon powdered sugar

Combine all ingredients and beat to soft peaks. Makes about ¾ cup.

Cinnamon Fireball Gelato

MAKES ABOUT 1 QUART

4 egg yolks

¾ cup sugar

2 cups whole milk

1 cup heavy cream

1 teaspoon ground cinnamon

2 tablespoons cinnamon schnapps

1 tablespoon light rum

Whipped cream, for garnish

Ground cinnamon, for garnish

This is the mellow baby sister of the Fireball Shooter, a fiery shot with rum, cinnamon schnapps, and Tabasco. For a ridiculously over-the-top sundae, serve a few scoops sprinkled with red hot candies, hot fudge sauce, and ground cinnamon.

1. Whisk the egg yolks and sugar in a large bowl. Set aside.
2. Combine the milk and cream in a medium-sized, heavy-bottomed pot. Cook over medium heat, stirring occasionally, until the edges just start to bubble. Remove the pot from the heat.
3. Slowly, drizzle the hot mixture into the egg yolk mixture, whisking constantly. Return the mixture to the pot. Cook over medium heat, whisking constantly, until it registers 170°F on a candy thermometer and is thick enough to coat the back of a spoon.
4. Strain the mixture into a large bowl. Stir in the ground cinnamon, cinnamon schnapps, and light rum. Cool in an ice bath, whisking frequently to lower the mixture's temperature. Refrigerate until completely chilled, about 4–6 hours.
5. Process the mixture in your ice cream maker according to the manufacturer's instructions. Transfer to a container and freeze overnight.
6. Serve garnished with whipped cream and a dusting of ground cinnamon.

Pistachio Rum Gelato

MAKES ABOUT 1 QUART

1½ cups unsalted pistachios, shelled

4 egg yolks

1 cup sugar

2 cups whole milk

1 cup heavy cream

¼ cup light rum

Whipped cream, for garnish

Shelled pistachios, for garnish

Warning: This ain't your average scoop of bright green pistachio. Toasting the pistachios really helps to bring out their flavor. If you can't survive without that neon-green color, feel free to play mad scientist and stir some all-natural, green food coloring into the custard as it cools.

1. Put the pistachios in a nonstick pan on the stove over medium heat. Toast, stirring frequently, until fragrant and lightly browned. Remove from heat and transfer to a plate. Cool to room temperature.

2. Put the toasted pistachios in the bowl of your food processor. Pulse a few times to grind them. Don't overprocess them, or you'll wind up with pistachio butter. Set aside.

3. Whisk the egg yolks and the sugar in a large bowl. Set aside.

4. Combine the milk and cream in a medium-sized, heavy-bottomed pot. Cook over medium heat, stirring occasionally, until the edges just start to bubble. Remove the pot from the heat.

5. Slowly, drizzle the hot mixture into the egg yolk mixture, whisking constantly. Return the mixture to the pot. Cook over medium heat, whisking constantly, until it registers 170°F on a candy thermometer and is thick enough to coat the back of a spoon.

6. Strain the mixture into a large bowl. Stir in the rum and ground pistachios. Cool in an ice bath, whisking frequently to lower the mixture's temperature. Refrigerate until completely chilled, about 4–6 hours.

7. Process the mixture in your ice cream maker according to the manufacturer's instructions. Transfer to a container and freeze overnight.

8. Serve garnished with whipped cream and a few whole, shelled pistachios.

Chapter
5

Frozen Yogurt

Frozen yogurt, or *froyo*, is the quintessential summer treat because a lot of the recipes don't involve any cooking on the stove.

Simply put the yogurt in a big bowl, mix in a little sugar, maybe some cream, and whatever flavorings you like, then toss it in the ice cream maker and let the beast work its magic. It really is that easy. Stay as simple or get as fancy as you like with the flavorings. The hard part is waiting for it to freeze.

One of the great things about making frozen yogurt is that you can choose the kind of yogurt you put in it. Whole milk Greek yogurt makes ridiculously thick, creamy, luxurious froyo. Nonfat yogurt produces a thinner treat that's almost akin to old-fashioned ice milk—with plenty of tang.

Orange Creamsicle Frozen Yogurt with Grand Marnier

MAKES ABOUT 1 QUART

1 teaspoon unflavored gelatin

1½ cups freshly squeezed orange juice, strained

⅔ cup sugar

1 tablespoon honey

1½ cups plain, whole milk yogurt

2 tablespoons Grand Marnier

This frozen yogurt tastes just like an ice cream truck Creamsicle. It's rich and creamy, and just a little bit tangy. Fresh orange juice and triple sec give it a double shot of bright citrus flavor. A little gelatin adds body and contributes to the smooth texture—and helps it set up.

1. Put the gelatin in a medium saucepan. Add the orange juice. When you pour it in, the gelatin may clump up a little, so just give it a brisk whisking. Let the orange juice and gelatin sit like this for about 5 minutes.
2. Add the sugar and honey to the pot. Whisk to combine. Set the pot on the stove over high heat and bring it to a boil, whisking occasionally. Let the mixture boil for a minute or two. Remove the pot from the stove. Cool the mixture to room temperature, then stick it in the fridge to chill it completely. At this point, if you give the syrup a taste, it will be very sweet. It's okay because the flavors balance out when you add the yogurt later on.
3. When your orange syrup is totally cold, whisk in the yogurt and triple sec. Process the mixture in your ice cream maker according to the manufacturer's instructions.
4. When you're done, your frozen yogurt will still be fairly slushy in consistency. Transfer it to a freezer-safe container. Smooth the surface down and press a piece of plastic wrap onto the surface.
5. Pop the container into the freezer. Freeze overnight to firm the frozen yogurt up completely.

Matcha Frozen Yogurt with Green Tea Infusion

MAKES ABOUT 1½ QUARTS

⅔ cup vodka

1 tablespoon loose green tea

4 cups plain, whole milk Greek yogurt

1 cup sugar

3 tablespoons matcha green tea

Matcha is a powdered Japanese green tea. Its intense green tea flavor—and color—packs a Godzilla-sized punch. Homemade, green tea–infused vodka adds a little extra flavor and kick.

1. Start by making the infused vodka the day before you want to make your frozen yogurt. Combine the vodka and loose green tea in a clean glass jar. Shake well, cover, and leave on the counter to infuse overnight. Strain the next day, discarding the solids.
2. Combine the yogurt, sugar, matcha, and ¼ cup of the green tea–infused vodka in a large bowl. Whisk together until the sugar is completely dissolved. Refrigerate until cold.
3. Process the mixture in your ice cream maker according to the manufacturer's instructions. Transfer to a container. Freeze overnight.

A Sparkling Ninja

This recipe makes a little more green–tea infused vodka than you actually need. Use the rest to make a killer drink, called a Sparkling Ninja!

1. Fill a rocks glass half full with ice.
2. Add a shot of green tea–infused vodka.
3. Fill with ginger ale.
4. Garnish with a cucumber wedge.

Drunken Goddess Frozen Yogurt

MAKES ABOUT 1 QUART

3 cups plain, whole milk Greek yogurt

1 cup heavy cream

Zest from 1 large lemon

¾ cup honey

¼ cup Drambuie

This ridiculously thick and luxurious treat is made with Greek yogurt, lemon zest, and honey. It's quite possibly the closest thing you'll find to ambrosia and nectar this side of Mount Olympus.

1. Put the yogurt, cream, lemon zest, honey, and Drambuie in a large bowl. Mix until completely uniform. Refrigerate until cold.
2. Process the mixture in your ice cream maker according to the manufacturer's instructions. Transfer to a container. Freeze overnight.

Pumpkin Pie Frozen Yogurt with Spiced Rum

MAKES ABOUT 1½ QUARTS

3 cups plain, whole milk Greek yogurt

1½ cups canned pumpkin

1 cup sugar

¼ teaspoon ground cinnamon

¼ teaspoon ground cloves

¼ teaspoon ground nutmeg

¼ teaspoon allspice

¼ cup Kraken spiced rum

Pumpkin pie isn't just for Thanksgiving. Enjoy it year-round in this version of spiced pumpkin pie—in creamy, frozen yogurt form.

1. Combine all ingredients in a large bowl. Whisk well until uniform. Refrigerate until cold.
2. Process the mixture in your ice cream maker according to the manufacturer's instructions. Transfer to a container. Freeze overnight.

> *Know Your Canned Pumpkin* You can find canned pumpkin in the baking aisle of most major grocery stores. But, buyer beware. Always get 100-percent pumpkin purée—NOT canned pumpkin pie filling, which comes preloaded with sugar and spices. Using the straight purée lets you control the sweetness and flavor.

Madras Frozen Yogurt

MAKES ABOUT 1 QUART

1 cup dried cranberries or Craisins

5 tablespoons orange juice

3 cups plain, whole milk Greek yogurt

1 cup whole cranberries (fresh or frozen)

1 cup sugar

1 cup cranberry juice

Zest from 1 large orange

¼ cup triple sec

This frozen yogurt combines all the flavors of a classic Madras cocktail. Made with puréed cranberries and studded with dried fruit, it will definitely satisfy your cranberry cravings.

1. Put the dried cranberries in a small bowl. Add the orange juice and 1 tablespoon of triple sec. Toss to combine. Cover and refrigerate overnight to plump up.
2. Put the yogurt, whole cranberries, sugar, and cranberry juice in the blender. Blend until smooth. Strain into a bowl. Whisk in the orange zest and the remaining 3 tablespoons of triple sec. Refrigerate until cold.
3. Process the mixture in your ice cream maker according to the manufacturer's instructions, adding in the orange juice and triple sec–infused dried cranberries in the last 5 minutes. Transfer to a container. Freeze overnight.

Triple Ginger Brandy Frozen Yogurt

MAKES ABOUT 1 QUART

4 cups plain, whole milk Greek yogurt

½ cup superfine sugar

Zest from 1 large lemon

1 tablespoon ground ginger

¼ cup Domaine de Canton ginger liqueur

½ cup candied ginger, chopped

This froyo gets a triple dose of fiery ginger flavor from ground ginger, candied ginger, and ginger liqueur.

1. Put the yogurt, superfine sugar, lemon zest, ground ginger, and ginger liqueur in a large bowl. Mix until completely uniform. Refrigerate until cold.
2. Process the mixture in your ice cream maker according to the manufacturer's instructions, adding in the chopped candied ginger in the last 5 minutes. Transfer to a container. Freeze overnight.

Sex on the Beach Frozen Yogurt

MAKES ABOUT 1 QUART

3 cups plain, whole milk Greek yogurt

1 cup cranberry juice

Zest from 1 large orange

¾ cup sugar

2 tablespoons vodka

2 tablespoons peach schnapps

¼ cup maraschino cherries, chopped finely

There are a zillion different recipes for Sex on the Beach. This is a frozen yogurt take on my version, made with cranberry, orange, and peach. Chopped maraschino cherries add a little texture, color, and an extra kiss of sweetness.

1. Put the yogurt, cranberry juice, orange zest, sugar, vodka, and peach schnapps in a large bowl. Mix until completely uniform. Refrigerate until cold.
2. Process the mixture in your ice cream maker according to the manufacturer's instructions, adding in the chopped maraschino cherries in the last 5 minutes. Transfer to a container. Freeze overnight.

Classic Piña Colada Frozen Yogurt

MAKES ABOUT 1 QUART

3 cups plain, whole milk Greek yogurt

1 cup coconut milk

¾ cup sugar

4 tablespoons light rum

¼ cup fresh, ripe pineapple, chopped finely

A classic piña colada is a simple concoction of pineapple, rum, and coconut milk. This tangy frozen version is shot through with bits of fresh, chopped pineapple. In a pinch, use unsweetened, strained, canned pineapple.

1. Put the yogurt, coconut milk, sugar, and rum in a large bowl. Mix until completely uniform. Refrigerate until cold.
2. Process the mixture in your ice cream maker according to the manufacturer's instructions, adding in the chopped pineapple in the last 5 minutes. Transfer to a container. Freeze overnight.

Maple Bourbon Yogurt Studded with Bacon & Pecans

MAKES ABOUT 1 QUART

3 strips uncooked bacon

½ cup pecans

4 cups plain, whole milk Greek yogurt

¾ cup pure maple syrup

¼ teaspoon natural maple extract

¼ cup bourbon

Mmm, mmm, mmm. Talk about a bunch of flavors that were meant to be together. This rich frozen yogurt gets its intense maple flavor from pure maple syrup and a little maple extract. Bits of salty bacon add a little crunch—and great contrast. Bourbon and toasted pecans seal the deal.

1. Bake the bacon on a parchment-lined sheet pan at 400°F until crisp (about 15 minutes), flipping it over about halfway through cooking. Drain, cool, and chop into bits. Set aside.
2. Toast the pecans on the stove in a skillet over medium heat, stirring often. They're done after about 5 minutes, when they're lightly browned and very fragrant. Remove from pan, cool, and chop into bits. Set aside.
3. Put the yogurt, maple syrup, maple extract, and bourbon in a large bowl. Mix until completely uniform. Refrigerate until cold.
4. Process the mixture in your ice cream maker according to the manufacturer's instructions, adding the chopped bacon and pecans in the last 5 minutes. Transfer to a container. Freeze overnight.

Limoncello Swirl Frozen Yogurt

MAKES ABOUT 1 QUART

4 cups plain, whole milk Greek yogurt

¼ cup sugar

Zest from 1 large lemon

¼ cup Limoncello

¾ cup lemon curd

Calling all lemon lovers! With lemon zest, Limoncello, and a hefty swirl of lemon curd, this frozen yogurt is sweet, tart—and long on lemony flavor. Adjust the amount of sugar up or down, depending on how sweet your lemon curd is.

1. Put the yogurt, sugar, lemon zest, and Limoncello in a large bowl. Mix until completely uniform. Refrigerate until cold.
2. Process the mixture in your ice cream maker according to the manufacturer's instructions. Transfer to a container. Spoon the lemon curd over the frozen yogurt and swirl it through with a butter knife. Freeze overnight.

Homemade Lemon Curd

Makes about 1 cup

If you use lemon curd purchased from a store, taste it before you start cooking and adjust the amount of sugar as necessary. Different brands have varying amounts of sweetness. For unbelievably fresh lemon flavor, you can also make your own.

3 egg yolks
½ cup sugar
Zest and juice of 2 large lemons
4 tablespoons butter

Cook the egg yolks, sugar, lemon zest, and lemon juice in the top of a double boiler for about 7 minutes, whisking frequently, until it's pale yellow, thickened, and registers 170°F on a candy thermometer. Remove from the heat and whisk in the butter 1 tablespoon at a time. Cool and refrigerate for up to 2 weeks.

Dirty Banana Frozen Yogurt

MAKES ABOUT 1 QUART

3–4 large, ripe whole bananas, peeled and cut into chunks

2 cups plain, whole milk Greek yogurt

¾ cup sugar

½ teaspoon vanilla extract

¼ cup Kahlua

⅛ teaspoon ground allspice

A dirty banana is an unlikely—and completely delicious—combination of banana and coffee-flavored liqueur. This frozen yogurt combines fresh bananas and Kahlua, with just a hint of allspice.

1. Put the bananas, yogurt, sugar, vanilla extract, Kahlua, and ground allspice in a blender. Blend until smooth. Refrigerate until cold.
2. Process the mixture in your ice cream maker according to the manufacturer's instructions. Transfer to a container. Freeze overnight.

Rusty Nail Frozen Yogurt

MAKES ABOUT 1 QUART

4 cups plain, whole milk Greek yogurt

Zest from 1 large lemon

¾ cup honey

1 teaspoon Drambuie

¼ cup Scotch

The Rusty Nail is a classic cocktail that's a heady combination of Scotch and honey-flavored Drambuie. Here's a frozen yogurt version, with just a smidge of lemon zest thrown in to balance out the flavors.

1. Put the yogurt, lemon zest, honey, Drambuie, and Scotch in a large bowl. Mix until completely uniform. Refrigerate until cold.
2. Process the mixture in your ice cream maker according to the manufacturer's instructions. Transfer to a container. Freeze overnight.

Strawberry Banana Daiquiri Frozen Yogurt

MAKES ABOUT 1 QUART

2 ripe whole bananas, peeled and cut into chunks

1 cup fresh strawberries, hulled and sliced

2 cups plain, whole milk Greek yogurt

¾ cup sugar

¼ cup light rum

Fresh strawberries and ripe bananas make this a really thick, fabulously fruity frozen yogurt. Minus the rum, it practically qualifies as health food. (Actually, leave out the rum and add a scoop of protein powder, and you'll have a supercharged, nonalcoholic smoothie.)

1. Put the bananas, strawberries, yogurt, sugar, and light rum in the blender. Blend until smooth. Refrigerate until cold.
2. Process the mixture in your ice cream maker according to the manufacturer's instructions. Transfer to a container. Freeze overnight.

Irish Coffee Frozen Yogurt

MAKES ABOUT 1 QUART

3 cups plain, whole milk Greek yogurt

1 cup strong brewed coffee, cold

¾ cup brown sugar

¼ cup whiskey

This high-octane frozen yogurt gets plenty of zip from freshly brewed coffee. Brown sugar and whiskey add hints of mellow caramel.

1. Put the yogurt, coffee, brown sugar, and whiskey in a large bowl. Mix until completely uniform. Refrigerate until cold.
2. Process the mixture in your ice cream maker according to the manufacturer's instructions. Transfer to a container. Freeze overnight.

Eggnog & Bourbon Frozen Yogurt

MAKES ABOUT 1 QUART

3 cups plain, whole milk Greek yogurt

1 cup eggnog

½ cup sugar

¼ cup bourbon

½ teaspoon freshly grated nutmeg

This is a great alternative to straight-up eggnog in the winter. Serve it as a lighter dessert after a rich holiday feast.

1. Put the yogurt, eggnog, sugar, bourbon, and grated nutmeg in a large bowl. Mix until completely uniform. Refrigerate until cold.
2. Process the mixture in your ice cream maker according to the manufacturer's instructions. Transfer to a container. Freeze overnight.

Chapter 6

Semifreddo, Mousse, and Parfaits

These frozen treats tend to be lighter and less dense than ice cream and gelato.

In Italian, *semifreddo* literally means "half cold," and the ones that you see are typically molded, with the texture of a frozen mousse. Because they incorporate a lot of whipped cream, they're very airy, and they tend to freeze less solidly than ice cream.

Technically, a parfait is any dessert that's served layered in a dish. Serve frozen parfaits in pretty glasses and goblets, so you can see the dessert.

Raspberry Liqueur Semifreddo

MAKES 10–12 SERVINGS

2 pints fresh raspberries, plus more for garnish

5 egg yolks

½ cup sugar

¼ cup raspberry liqueur

3 cups heavy cream

¼ cup seedless raspberry jam

Whipped cream, for garnish

Fresh mint, for garnish

This semifreddo would make a spectacular finale for a swanky dinner party. Lush raspberry-infused whipped cream is swirled with sweet raspberry jam, then crowned with fresh raspberries. The whole thing is frozen in a loaf pan, so it holds a nice shape. Serve fat slices garnished with whipped cream, fresh raspberries, and mint.

1. Line a one-pound loaf pan with plastic wrap. Spread half the raspberries on the bottom. Pop the pan in the freezer.
2. Whisk the egg yolks, sugar, and raspberry liqueur together. Cook in a double boiler, whisking constantly, until it reaches about 170°F and is thick enough to coat the back of a spoon. Remove from heat. Chill in an ice bath, then refrigerate until cold.
3. Beat the cream in your stand mixer until it forms soft peaks. In batches, fold the cold egg yolk mixture into the whipped cream. Fold in the rest of the fresh raspberries.
4. Pour the mixture into your prepared loaf pan. Spoon the raspberry jam on top of the mixture. With a knife, gently swirl the jam through the mixture.
5. Cover with plastic wrap, pressing it gently to the surface. Freeze overnight.
6. To unmold, remove the pan from the freezer and let it sit at room temperature for about 10 minutes to loosen up. Remove the top layer of plastic wrap. Invert the pan onto a serving platter. Remove the bottom layer of plastic wrap.
7. Slice with a warmed knife. (Run the knife under hot water for a minute, then dry before slicing.) Serve garnished with fresh raspberries and mint leaves.

Mocha Semifreddo with Kahlua & Shaved Chocolate

MAKES 10–12 SERVINGS

5 egg yolks

½ cup sugar

¼ cup Kahlua

½ cup strong brewed coffee, chilled

3 cups heavy cream

2 tablespoons unsweetened cocoa powder

2 tablespoons powdered sugar

Whipped cream, for garnish

Chocolate shavings, for garnish

Serve this with espresso after a big dinner with friends. Rich, coffee-laced whipped cream is spiked with Kahlua. Serve thick slices with whipped cream and chocolate shavings.

1. Line a one-pound loaf pan with plastic wrap. Set aside.
2. Whisk the egg yolks, sugar, Kahlua, and coffee together. Cook in a double boiler, whisking constantly, until it reaches about 170°F and is thick enough to coat the back of a spoon. Remove from heat. Chill in an ice bath, then refrigerate until cold.
3. Beat the cream, cocoa powder, and powdered sugar in your stand mixer until it forms soft peaks. In batches, fold the cold egg yolk mixture into the whipped cream.
4. Pour the mixture into your prepared loaf pan. Cover with plastic wrap, pressing it gently to the surface. Freeze overnight.
5. To unmold, remove the pan from the freezer and let it sit at room temperature for about 10 minutes to loosen up. Remove the top layer of plastic wrap. Invert the pan onto a serving platter. Remove the bottom layer of plastic wrap.
6. Slice with a warmed knife. (Run the knife under hot water for a minute, then dry before slicing.) Garnish with whipped cream and chocolate shavings.

Strawberry & Champagne Semifreddo

MAKES 10–12 SERVINGS

1½ pounds hulled strawberries, divided

¾ cup white sugar

Pinch of salt

¾ teaspoon fresh lemon juice

¼ cup champagne or prosecco

2 cups heavy cream

Additional strawberries, hulled and sliced, for garnish

Strawberries and champagne is a sweet and lovely combination. They pair nicely in a glass—or in this frozen mousse. This strawberry-topped dessert is sure to be a hit at your next brunch. Make it the night before for worry-free hosting.

1. Line a one-pound loaf pan with plastic wrap. Slice ⅓ of the strawberries and arrange them neatly in the bottom of the pan. Pop the pan into the freezer.
2. Roughly chop the remaining pound of berries. Put them in a medium-sized bowl with the sugar, salt, and lemon juice. Let the mixture sit on the counter for about 10 minutes.
3. Pour about half of the mixture into your blender. Blend until smooth. Combine the purée and the rest of the berry mixture in a bowl. Add the champagne or prosecco. Mix to combine well. Chill the mixture for 2–4 hours, or until cold.
4. Beat the cream to stiff peaks. Fold in the chilled berry mixture in thirds. Pour into prepared loaf pan. Press a piece of plastic wrap to the surface. Freeze overnight.
5. To unmold, remove the pan from the freezer and let it sit at room temperature for about 10 minutes to loosen up. Remove the top layer of plastic wrap. Invert the pan onto a serving platter. Remove the bottom layer of plastic wrap.
6. Slice with a warm knife and serve garnished with fresh strawberries.

Lady Godiva's Frozen Chocolate Mousse

MAKES ABOUT 1 QUART

1 teaspoon instant espresso powder

1 tablespoon hot water

4 ounces unsweetened chocolate, chopped

½ cup sweetened condensed milk

½ teaspoon vanilla extract

Pinch of salt

1 cup heavy cream

4 tablespoons Godiva chocolate liqueur

This light and airy mousse gets its poof from whipped cream that's been spiked with a liberal dose of chocolate liqueur. The condensed milk gives it the velvety texture—and adds subtle caramel notes.

1. Put the instant espresso powder in a small bowl. Add the hot water. Stir to dissolve. Set aside.
2. Put the chopped chocolate, condensed milk, dissolved espresso, vanilla extract, and salt in a large, microwave-safe bowl. Mix until uniform.
3. Melt the mixture in the microwave on high for a minute or two, stopping it every 10 or 20 seconds to stir. (If you don't have a microwave, use a double boiler.) Set aside.
4. Put the cream in a large mixing bowl of a stand mixer. Beat on high until it forms soft peaks. Add the chocolate liqueur and beat to incorporate.
5. Working in batches, fold the whipped cream into the chocolate mixture. (Be careful to not smoosh all the air out of the whipped cream.)
6. Transfer to a freezer-safe container. Freeze overnight.

Condensed Milk vs. Evaporated Milk What's the difference? In a word: sugar. And it's a huge difference. Condensed milk is whole milk that's been slow cooked with sugar until it's reduced by a little more than half. The result is thick, syrupy, and caramel flavored. Evaporated milk is thin and unsweetened. Make sure you walk out of the market with the right can. They're definitely not interchangeable.

Chocolate Espresso Martini Mousse

MAKES ABOUT 1 QUART

2 teaspoons instant espresso powder

2 tablespoons hot water

10 ounces semisweet chocolate chips

3 cups heavy cream

½ teaspoon vanilla extract

¼ cup espresso-flavored vodka

Like chocolate ganache? You'll love this mousse. It's basically a frozen, whipped ganache that's been infused with rich espresso, then laced with espresso-flavored vodka. Serve this rich mousse in small bowls with cups of steaming espresso.

1. Put the instant espresso in a small bowl. Add the hot water. Stir to dissolve. Set aside.
2. Put the chocolate chips in a large bowl. Heat the cream in a medium-sized, heavy-bottomed pot until it just starts to bubble at the edges. Pour the hot cream over the chocolate chips. Let stand for 5 minutes, then whisk until the chocolate melts and the mixture is uniform. Let cool to room temperature, then chill completely. This is the ganache.
3. Beat the chilled ganache until it holds soft peaks. Drizzle in the vanilla extract and vodka with the mixer running.
4. Transfer the chocolate mousse into a freezer-safe container. Smooth the top down with a spatula. Cover it with plastic wrap, pressing the plastic down so it covers the surface of the mousse. Pop the pan in the freezer for at least 6 hours, preferably overnight.

Orange Curaçao Parfait

MAKES 6–8 SERVINGS

4 egg yolks

½ cup sugar

½ cup freshly squeezed orange juice

Zest of 1 large orange + more for garnish

1 cup heavy cream

3 tablespoons orange curaçao

Whipped cream, for serving

This parfait is lighter than a traditional ice cream or gelato—but still plenty creamy. Serve it scooped in large goblets, layered with whipped cream and dusted with orange zest.

1. Beat the egg yolks, sugar, orange juice, and orange zest together in a large, heatproof bowl. Cook in a double boiler, whisking constantly, until the mixture reaches 165°F, about 7 minutes. Whatever you do, don't let it boil.
2. Remove from the heat. Continue to beat until cool, about another 7 minutes. Set aside.
3. Beat the cream and orange curaçao together until the mixture forms soft peaks. Gently fold the whipped cream into the egg mixture in thirds. Be sure to fold gently, so you don't de-poof your whipped cream.
4. Transfer the parfait to a bowl. Cover with plastic wrap and freeze overnight.

Penny's Pumpkin Parfait with Spiced Rum

MAKES 6–8 SERVINGS

1½ cups canned pumpkin

¾ cup brown sugar

1 teaspoon ground cinnamon

1 teaspoon ground ginger

¼ teaspoon ground cloves

3 cups heavy cream

¼ cup spiced rum

Whipped cream, for serving

Molasses cookies, for serving

Hello, pumpkin perfection! Named after one of our pups, this parfait makes a great end to a holiday meal. Serve layered with whipped cream and crumbled molasses cookies.

1. Whisk the pumpkin, brown sugar, ground cinnamon, ground ginger, and ground cloves together in a large bowl until uniform.
2. Beat the cream in a large bowl or the bowl of your stand mixer until it forms soft peaks. Beat in the spiced rum until incorporated.
3. Working in batches, gently fold the whipped cream into the pumpkin mixture, being careful not to deflate it.
4. Transfer to a bowl. Cover with plastic wrap. Freeze overnight.

Know Your Canned Pumpkin You can find canned pumpkin in the baking aisle of most major grocery stores. But, buyer beware. Always get 100-percent pumpkin purée—NOT canned pumpkin pie filling, which comes preloaded with sugar and spices. Using the straight purée lets you control the sweetness and flavor—and skip extra preservatives.

S'mores Martini Parfait

**MAKES ABOUT 1 QUART,
SERVES 6–8**

3½ cups mini marshmallows,
divided

¼ cup unsweetened cocoa powder

2½ cups heavy cream, divided

3 tablespoons vodka

1 tablespoon chocolate liqueur

Mini chocolate chips, for serving

Graham crackers, for serving

Whipped cream, for serving

This one's for all you former Girl Scouts and Brownies out there. S'mores are a classic campfire treat. In this grown-up version, a rich chocolate parfait is studded with mini marshmallows and laced with vodka and chocolate liqueur.

1. Melt 2½ cups of mini marshmallows and ½ cup cream in a double boiler, whisking constantly until the mixture is smooth and uniform. Remove from the heat. Whisk in the vodka and chocolate liqueur. Cool to room temperature.
2. Combine the remaining 2 cups of cream and the cocoa powder in a large bowl and beat to soft peaks. Working in batches, fold the whipped cream into the cooled chocolate mixture. Fold in the remaining 1 cup of mini marshmallows.
3. Transfer to a bowl. Cover with plastic wrap and freeze overnight.
4. Serve layered with mini chocolate chips, crushed graham crackers, and whipped cream.

Chapter 7

Granita

Granita is sweetened, shaved ice that makes an elegant, light dessert—or pre-dinner cocktail. It's super simple to make. All you need is a lasagna pan, a freezer, and a fork.

The only downside to granita is that you have to be around to tend it. It needs to be raked every half hour or so. That said, it takes maybe 3 minutes each time, so you can easily make it while you're doing other stuff. Plan on 3–4 hours from start to finish.

Make granita with any kind of sweetened liquid, from fruit juice to wine—and pretty much anything in between. Here's the basic technique.

GRANITA 101

1. Prepare the granita mixture according to your recipe.
2. Pour it into a wide, shallow pan. 9" × 13" baking dishes work really well. Just be sure your dish is freezer-safe and you have the room in the freezer.
3. Pop the pan into the freezer for about an hour.
4. After an hour, it will start to freeze around the edges. Yank the pan out of the freezer and rake the ice crystals around with a fork. Return it to the freezer.
5. Continue to rake the mixture with a fork every 30 minutes, until the entire mixture is icy and frozen.
6. To serve, scoop the icy crystals into glass goblets or martini glasses. It will start to melt almost immediately, so serve it right away. You can also scoop your granita ahead of time and pop the goblets or glasses back into the freezer.

Blood Orange Vodka Granita

MAKES ABOUT 1 QUART

1 cup water

1 cup sugar

3½ cups freshly squeezed blood orange juice (from about 12–14 blood oranges)

¼ cup vodka

Blood oranges are a variety of orange with a blushing red rind and cherry-colored flesh. The freshly squeezed juice makes for a luscious, crimson granita that tastes faintly of raspberries.

1. Put the water and sugar in a medium-sized pot over high heat. Simmer until the sugar has dissolved. Cool to room temperature.
2. Whisk in the blood orange juice and vodka.
3. Pour into a shallow, freezer-safe dish. Freeze for an hour. Stir the mixture with a fork to break it up. Return to the freezer. Check and rake with a fork every 30 minutes, until the entire mixture is icy and frozen.

Black Russian Granita

MAKES ABOUT 1 QUART

4 cups strong brewed coffee, hot

1¼ cups light brown sugar

3 tablespoons vodka

1 tablespoon Kahlua

This take on a classic Black Russian cocktail is made with freshly brewed coffee and a generous amount of vodka and Kahlua. Brown sugar adds unexpected caramel notes. This recipe calls for light brown sugar, but if you want a stronger molasses flavor, substitute dark brown sugar.

1. Whisk the brown sugar into the hot coffee until dissolved. Cool to room temperature.
2. Stir in the vodka and Kahlua.
3. Pour into a shallow, freezer-safe dish. Freeze for an hour. Stir the mixture with a fork to break it up. Return to the freezer. Check and rake with a fork every 30 minutes, until the entire mixture is icy and frozen.

Tipsy Witch Granita Infused with Rosemary & Lemon

MAKES ABOUT 1 QUART

2 cups water

1 cup sugar

5 large sprigs fresh rosemary

Zest from 1 large lemon

1 cup fresh lemon juice

¼ cup Strega liqueur

Rosemary-infused simple syrup, fresh lemon zest and juice, and Strega liqueur make this taste like an herbal Italian ice. This recipe is inspired by my friends here in Salem, Massachusetts, which is an absolutely magical place to live.

1. Put the sugar and water in a medium-sized pot. Bring to a boil and whisk until the sugar completely dissolves. Remove from heat. Toss in the rosemary and lemon zest. Cover the pot. Let the syrup infuse, covered, until it cools to room temperature, about 60 minutes. Strain and discard the solids.
2. Stir in the fresh lemon juice and Strega.
3. Pour into a shallow, freezer-safe dish. Freeze for an hour. Stir the mixture with a fork to break it up. Return to the freezer. Check and rake with a fork every 30 minutes, until the entire mixture is icy and frozen.

Quick Tip If you don't have fresh rosemary (or are having a granita emergency), substitute 3 tablespoons of dried herb.

What Is Strega Liqueur? Strega is an Italian herbal liqueur made in Benevento with 70 ingredients, including saffron, mint, and fennel. *Strega* is also Italian for *witch*.

Hot & Spicy Bloody Mary Granita

MAKES ABOUT 1 QUART

4 cups tomato juice

½ teaspoon sriracha

½ teaspoon freshly grated horseradish

2 tablespoons fresh parsley, chopped

2 tablespoons fresh lemon juice

¼ teaspoon kosher salt

¼ teaspoon freshly ground black pepper

¼ teaspoon ground celery seed

½ teaspoon Worcestershire sauce

¼ cup vodka

This granita gets its heat from sriracha, a spicy Asian hot sauce, and freshly grated horseradish. For a milder version, cut down on the amounts—or omit them entirely. For a five-alarm treat, increase the amount of sriracha to 1 teaspoon. (And don't say I didn't warn you.)

1. Whisk all ingredients together until well combined. Give the mixture a taste, and adjust the seasoning as necessary.
2. Pour into a shallow, freezer-safe dish. Freeze for an hour. Stir the mixture with a fork to break it up. Return to the freezer. Check and rake with a fork every 30 minutes, until the entire mixture is icy and frozen.

Quick Tip If you don't have ground celery seed, substitute ¼ teaspoon celery salt and leave out the kosher salt.

Sweet Shiraz Granita

MAKES ABOUT 1 QUART

1 cup water

¾ cup sugar

Zest from 1 large orange

3 cups Shiraz

This granita is sweet and jammy. Make it with your favorite Shiraz or other full-bodied red wine.

1. Put the water, sugar, and orange zest in a medium-sized pot. Bring to a boil and whisk until the sugar completely dissolves. Remove from heat. Cool to room temperature.
2. Stir in the Shiraz.
3. Pour into a shallow, freezer-safe dish. Freeze for an hour. Stir the mixture with a fork to break it up. Return to the freezer. Check and rake with a fork every 30 minutes, until the entire mixture is icy and frozen.

Strawberry Sangria Granita

MAKES ABOUT 1 QUART

1 cup water

1 cup sugar

Zest from 1 large orange

Zest from 1 large lemon

1 Granny Smith apple, peeled, cored, and chopped

1 cup fresh strawberries, hulled and chopped

3 cups Merlot

Fresh strawberries, sliced, for garnish

Do a quick recipe search, and you can find dozens of recipes for sangria, that heady Spanish concoction of wine, fruit, and sugar. This red wine sangria makes good use of ripe, early summer strawberries.

1. Put the water and sugar in a medium-sized pot on the stove. Bring to a boil and whisk until the sugar dissolves. Remove from heat. Toss in the orange zest, lemon zest, apple, and strawberries. Stir to combine. Cover and let the mixture infuse until it cools to room temperature, about 1 hour. Strain and discard the solids.
2. Stir in the Merlot.
3. Pour into a shallow, freezer-safe dish. Freeze for an hour. Stir the mixture with a fork to break it up. Return to the freezer. Check and rake with a fork every 30 minutes, until the entire mixture is icy and frozen.
4. Garnish with fresh, sliced strawberries.

Negroni & Orange Slush

MAKES ABOUT 1 QUART

4 cups orange juice

1 cup sugar

1½ tablespoons gin

1½ tablespoons Campari

1½ tablespoons sweet vermouth

Ginger ale, for serving

This take on a Negroni cocktail combines equal parts of the traditional gin, sweet vermouth, and Campari with a base of sweet orange juice to balance out the herbal flavors of the bitters and gin. To serve, scoop into glasses and top with a splash of ginger ale.

1. Combine the orange juice and sugar in a medium-sized pot. Simmer over medium-high heat, whisking constantly, until the sugar dissolves. Transfer to a bowl. Cool to room temperature.
2. Stir in the gin, Campari, and sweet vermouth.
3. Pour into a shallow, freezer-safe dish. Freeze for an hour. Stir the mixture with a fork to break it up. Return to the freezer. Check and rake with a fork every 30 minutes, until the entire mixture is icy and frozen.

Bailey's Irish Cream Granita

MAKES ABOUT 1 QUART

4 cups strong brewed coffee, hot

¾ cup sugar

⅔ cup Bailey's Irish Cream liqueur

If you're looking for a little hair of the dog on a hot summer morning, this could be just the ticket. It's sweet, caffeinated, and laced with just enough Bailey's Irish Cream.

1. Combine the hot coffee and sugar in a large bowl and whisk until the sugar completely dissolves. Cool to room temperature.
2. Stir in the Bailey's.
3. Pour into a shallow, freezer-safe dish. Freeze for an hour. Stir the mixture with a fork to break it up. Return to the freezer. Check and rake with a fork every 30 minutes, until the entire mixture is icy and frozen.

St. Germaine & Limoncello Granita

MAKES ABOUT 1 QUART

3 cups water

1 cup sugar

Zest of 1 large lemon

¼ cup fresh lemon juice

3 tablespoons St. Germaine, plus more for garnish

1 tablespoon Limoncello

Lemon twist

Elderflower-based St. Germaine and sunny Limoncello make for a bright, vibrant granita. To serve, scoop into martini glasses and top with a drizzle of St. Germaine. Garnish with a lemon twist for a pretty presentation.

1. Put the water and sugar in a medium-sized pot. Bring to a boil and whisk until the sugar completely dissolves. Remove from heat. Stir in the lemon zest. Cool to room temperature. Strain.
2. Stir in the lemon juice, St. Germaine, and Limoncello.
3. Pour into a shallow, freezer-safe dish. Freeze for an hour. Stir the mixture with a fork to break it up. Return to the freezer. Check and rake with a fork every 30 minutes, until the entire mixture is icy and frozen.

Shirley's Temple of Doom Granita

MAKES ABOUT 1 QUART

2 cups orange juice

1 tablespoon sugar

2 cups ginger ale

½ cup maraschino cherries, finely chopped

2 tablespoons grenadine syrup

¼ cup of maraschino liqueur

The inspiration for this one comes from my friend Kristyn, who loves Indiana Jones and drinks "adult" Shirley Temples spiked with cherry vodka and maraschino liqueur. It's a sweet and utterly sinful frozen take on the favorite childhood classic.

1. Whisk the orange juice and sugar together in a bowl until the sugar dissolves. Stir in the ginger ale, chopped maraschino cherries, grenadine, and maraschino liqueur.
2. Pour into a shallow, freezer-safe dish. Freeze for an hour. Stir the mixture with a fork to break it up. Return to the freezer. Check and rake with a fork every 30 minutes, until the entire mixture is icy and frozen.

Cuba Libre Granita

MAKES ABOUT 1 QUART

4 cups cola

¼ cup light rum

Zest from 2 large limes

The Cuba Libre, a.k.a. the infamous Rum and Coke, makes a fizzy, refreshing granita. Think of it kind of like a supercharged slushy.

1. Combine the cola and rum in a shallow, freezer-safe dish.
2. Gently stir in the lime zest. Freeze for an hour.
3. Stir the mixture with a fork to break it up. Return to the freezer.
4. Check and rake with a fork every 30 minutes, until the entire mixture is icy and frozen.

Southern Comfort & Peach Granita

MAKES ABOUT 1 QUART

4 cups peach nectar

¼ cup Southern Comfort

2 tablespoons fresh lemon juice

Southern Comfort is a classic liquor with hints of bourbon and peach. It's the perfect foil for sweet peach nectar. Serve straight up in glasses, or topped with a splash of ginger ale.

1. Whisk the peach nectar, Southern Comfort, and lemon juice together in a large bowl. Give it a taste. Depending on how sweet your peach nectar is, you may want to whisk in a few tablespoons of sugar.
2. Pour into a shallow, freezer-safe dish. Freeze for an hour. Stir the mixture with a fork to break it up. Return to the freezer. Check and rake with a fork every 30 minutes, until the entire mixture is icy and frozen.

Sloe Gin Fizz Granita

MAKES ABOUT 1 QUART

1 cup water

1 cup sugar

3 cups soda water

¼ cup sloe gin

2 tablespoons fresh lemon juice

This lovely pink granita is a fun twist for the gin lover in your life. Sloe gin, a shockingly red liqueur, is made by infusing blackthorn berries and sugar with gin. Serve this granita garnished with a lemon twist.

1. Put the water and sugar in a medium-sized pot over high heat. Simmer until the sugar has dissolved. Cool to room temperature.
2. Stir in the soda water, sloe gin, and lemon juice.
3. Pour into a shallow, freezer-safe dish. Freeze for an hour. Stir the mixture with a fork to break it up. Return to the freezer. Check and rake with a fork every 30 minutes, until the entire mixture is icy and frozen.

Moscow Mule Granita

MAKES ABOUT 1 QUART

4 cups ginger ale

¼ cup vodka

Zest from 1 large lemon

Candied ginger, for garnish

A Moscow Mule is a potent mix of ginger ale and vodka. This frozen version is long on ginger flavor. Garnish with a few slices of candied ginger.

1. Combine the ginger ale and vodka in a shallow, freezer-safe dish. Gently stir in the lemon zest. Freeze for an hour. Stir the mixture with a fork to break it up. Return to the freezer. Check and rake with a fork every 30 minutes, until the entire mixture is icy and frozen. Serve garnished with candied ginger.

How about a Slushy? Granitas make a great base for cocktails, since they're basically highly flavored ice. For a Moscow Mule Slushy, put a few scoops of granita into a martini glass. Toss on a shot or two of vodka and top with a splash of cold ginger ale.

Vodka Gimlet Granita

MAKES ABOUT 1 QUART

4 cups lemon-lime soda

¼ cup vodka

Zest and juice from 1 large lime

Zest and juice from 1 large lemon

This is a great treat to serve instead of cocktails at summer dinner parties. It's a sweet—and unexpected—way to start a meal on a warm August night.

1. Combine the lemon-lime soda, vodka, lemon juice, and lime juice in a shallow, freezer-safe dish. Gently stir in the lemon zest and lime zest. Freeze for an hour. Stir the mixture with a fork to break it up. Return to the freezer. Check and rake with a fork every 30 minutes, until the entire mixture is icy and frozen.

Chapter 8

Sorbet and Sherbet

What's the difference between sorbet and sherbet? It depends who you ask. In fact, some will tell you that the jury is still out. However, it's generally agreed upon that sherbets are made with milk, and sorbets are not.

Sorbets are typically a heady blend of fruit juices, sugar, and—in these recipes—some kind of alcohol. They can be smooth, or dotted with bits of fruit. They're a great way to use any kind of really ripe fruit you happen to have on hand. Don't be afraid to hit your local farmers' market and get creative with your blender.

While the few sherbets included here are creamy, keep in mind that they're going to be a lot icier than any kind of ice cream, because of the dramatically lower fat content and lack of egg yolks.

Because of the lower fat content in all the recipes in this section, take them out of the freezer about 15 minutes before you want to serve them. This will knock the chill off and make them nice and scoopable.

Blackberry Limoncello Sorbet

MAKES ABOUT 1 QUART

1¼ cups sugar

1 cup water

24 ounces fresh blackberries, plus more for garnish

1 tablespoon fresh lemon juice

¼ cup Limoncello

Lemon zest, for garnish

For this sorbet, sunny lemon Limoncello enhances the flavor of ripe, juicy blackberries. Serve big bowls garnished with a handful of fresh blackberries and a little lemon zest.

1. Combine the sugar and water in a medium-sized saucepan. Set the pot on the stove over high heat. Whisk occasionally until the sugar dissolves. Bring the mixture to a boil and continue boiling for about 2 minutes. This is now the simple syrup.
2. Remove the pot from the heat. Cool the mixture to room temperature, then pop it in the fridge to chill it completely.
3. Pick through your blackberries and discard any that are bruised or otherwise suspect looking. Put half of them in the blender along with half of the chilled simple syrup. Purée on high for 30 seconds, until the berries are completely liquefied.
4. Strain the blackberry mixture into a large bowl. It'll be thick, so push it through with a rubber spatula or wooden spoon.
5. Blend and strain the remaining blackberries and simple syrup. Add the lemon juice and Limoncello into the strained mixture. Stir to combine.
6. Because you chilled the simple syrup, your mixture should still be fairly cold. Process it in your ice cream maker according to the manufacturer's instructions.
7. When it's done, it will have the texture of melted ice cream. Transfer it to a freezer-safe container.
8. Smooth out the surface. Press a layer of plastic wrap onto the surface. Pop the pan into the freezer for at least a few hours (ideally, overnight), until it's completely frozen.

Cranberry Mulled Wine Sorbet

MAKES ABOUT 1 QUART

1½ cups freshly squeezed orange juice

1½ cups sugar

2½ cups whole cranberries

Zest from 1 orange

¼ teaspoon ground cinnamon

2 cups red zinfandel

Mulled wine is a popular fall cocktail. This zinfandel-infused orange cranberry sorbet is fragrant with cinnamon and freshly grated orange zest. The fresh cranberry reduction gives this sorbet a velvety, jammy texture. This recipe calls for a large amount of wine, so it freezes on the softer side. For a firmer sorbet, cut the wine down a little and up the amount of orange juice.

1. Put the orange juice and sugar in a medium-sized pot. Bring to a simmer over medium heat, whisking until the sugar dissolves. Add the cranberries. Continue to simmer, stirring frequently, until the cranberries start to pop open. Strain the mixture into a large bowl, mashing the solids down with a spoon to extract as much liquid as you can. Discard the solids.
2. Add the orange zest, ground cinnamon, and red zinfandel, stirring to combine. Let cool to room temperature, then chill completely in the fridge.
3. Process the mixture in your ice cream maker according to the manufacturer's instructions. Transfer to a container. Freeze overnight.

Lemon Drop Sorbet

MAKES ABOUT 1 QUART

2¼ cups water

¾ cup sugar

Zest from 1 lemon

¾ cup fresh lemon juice

¼ cup Absolut Citron vodka

Remember Lemonheads—the candy from when you were a kid? This sorbet is a version of their older sister, the Lemon Drop cocktail. It's a little sweet, a little sour, and packed with sassy lemon flavor.

1. Put the water and sugar in a medium-sized pot. Simmer over medium-high heat until the sugar dissolves. Remove from heat.
2. Stir in the lemon zest, lemon juice, and vodka. Let cool to room temperature, then chill in the fridge until completely cold.
3. Process the mixture in your ice cream maker according to the manufacturer's instructions. Transfer to a container. Freeze overnight.

Persephone's Pomegranate & Orange Liqueur Sorbet

MAKES ABOUT 1 QUART

2¼ cups pomegranate juice

½ cup sugar

Zest from 1 orange

¾ cup fresh orange juice

¼ cup PAMA pomegranate liqueur

This jewel-red sorbet is lush with ripe pomegranate flavor. A little orange juice and zest add bright citrus notes. A big bowl of this on a hot day is well worth a trip to the underworld (or supermarket).

1. Put the pomegranate juice and sugar in a medium-sized pot. Simmer over medium-high heat until the sugar dissolves. Remove from heat.
2. Stir in the orange zest, orange juice, and PAMA liqueur. Let cool to room temperature, then chill in the fridge until completely cold.
3. Process the mixture in your ice cream maker according to the manufacturer's instructions. Transfer to a container. Freeze overnight.

Quick Tips If you can't find PAMA liqueur, use Absolut Citron vodka or triple sec. Bottled pomegranate juice is available in the refrigerated section of most large U.S. markets. Use 100-percent juice, not a watered-down juice drink that's packed with sugar.

Limoncello & Mint Sorbet

MAKES ABOUT 1 QUART

2¼ cups water

¾ cup sugar

1 cup fresh mint leaves, packed

½ cup fresh lemon juice

¼ cup Limoncello

¼ cup fresh mint, finely chopped

This sorbet combines fresh mint and lemony Limoncello. It makes a great after-dinner palate cleanser.

1. Put the water and sugar in a medium-sized pot. Simmer over medium-high heat until the sugar dissolves. Stir in the fresh mint leaves. Remove from heat. Cover and let cool to room temperature. Strain into a bowl, discarding the solids.
2. Stir in the lemon juice and Limoncello. Let cool to room temperature, then chill in the fridge until completely cold.
3. Process the mixture in your ice cream maker according to the manufacturer's instructions, adding in the ¼ cup of chopped mint in the last 5 minutes. Transfer to a container. Freeze overnight.

Raspberry & Chambord Sorbet

MAKES ABOUT 1 QUART

1 cup pinot grigio

¾ cup sugar

5 cups fresh raspberries

Juice of ½ lemon

3 tablespoons Chambord

Fresh raspberries, for garnish

Fresh mint, for garnish

Serve scoops of this ruby-red sorbet in martini glasses, garnished with a few fresh raspberries and a sprig of mint.

1. Put the pinot grigio and sugar in a medium-sized pot. Simmer, whisking occasionally, until the sugar dissolves. Add the raspberries. Simmer for 5–10 minutes, stirring frequently, until the raspberries break down.
2. Remove pot from the heat. Strain mixture into a bowl, smooshing the raspberries down with a spoon to extract as much liquid as you can. Discard the solids.
3. Add the lemon juice and Chambord. Let cool to room temperature, then pop the bowl into the fridge to chill completely.
4. Process the mixture in your ice cream maker according to the manufacturer's instructions. Transfer to a container. Freeze overnight.

Harvey Wallbanger Sorbet

MAKES ABOUT 1 QUART

3 cups freshly squeezed orange juice

¾ cup sugar

Zest from 1 large orange

1 tablespoon triple sec

2 tablespoons vodka

1 tablespoon Galliano

The Harvey Wallbanger is one of those classic cocktails from the '50s that makes you feel like you should be in a ritzy hotel bar wearing a tailored pantsuit—and a fancy little hat. This smooth interpretation gets its kick from vodka, Galliano, and triple sec.

1. Put the orange juice, sugar, and orange zest in a medium-sized pot. Cook over medium heat, whisking constantly, until the sugar dissolves. Remove from heat, transfer to a bowl, and cool to room temperature.
2. Stir in the triple sec, vodka, and Galliano. Chill the mixture completely in the fridge.
3. Process the mixture in your ice cream maker according to the manufacturer's instructions. Transfer to a container. Freeze overnight.

Peach Champagne Sorbet

MAKES ABOUT 1 QUART

¼ cup sugar

2½ cups peach nectar

1½ cups champagne or prosecco

Talk about simple. With only three ingredients, this sorbet is elegant and easy to make. Serve with ripe, sliced peaches and a tall, icy glass of sparkling wine.

1. Put the peach nectar and sugar in a medium-sized pot. Simmer over medium heat, whisking occasionally, until the sugar dissolves. Remove from heat and transfer to a bowl. Cool to room temperature on the counter.
2. Stir in the champagne or prosecco. Chill in the fridge until completely cold.
3. Process the mixture in your ice cream maker according to the manufacturer's instructions. Transfer to a container. Freeze overnight.

Kirsch-Infused Slippery Cherry Sherbet

MAKES ABOUT 1½ QUARTS

3 cups whole milk

¾ cup sugar

¼ cup kirsch

¼ teaspoon almond extract

2 cups cherries, stemmed, pitted, and chopped

This sherbet is milky and sweet, with fresh cherry juice and just a hint of almond extract. Garnish with a maraschino cherry and/or a handful of toasted, chopped walnuts.

1. Put the milk and sugar in a medium-sized pot. Cook over medium heat, whisking constantly, until the sugar dissolves. Remove from heat, transfer to a bowl, and cool to room temperature.
2. Stir in the kirsch and almond extract. Chill the mixture completely in the fridge.
3. In your blender, purée the chilled mixture with the cherries.
4. Process the mixture in your ice cream maker according to the manufacturer's instructions. Transfer to a container. Freeze overnight.

A Killer Cherry Cocktail
For a killer frozen cherry cocktail, blend 3 cups of this sherbet, 1 cup of milk, and an extra shot or two of kirsch.

Black Magic Sorbet

MAKES ABOUT 1 QUART

¾ cup water

¾ cup sugar

1 whole vanilla bean

Zest from ½ large lemon

3½ cups strong brewed coffee, chilled

3 tablespoons vodka

1 tablespoon Kahlua

Chocolate-covered espresso beans, for garnish

Here's a frosty take on the Black Magic cocktail, a high-test combination of vodka, Kahlua, and coffee that's finished with a few dashes of lemon juice.

1. Put the water and sugar in a medium-sized pot. Split the vanilla bean lengthwise with a sharp knife. Scrape the paste out with the back of the knife. Add the vanilla paste and pod to the pot. Cook over medium heat, whisking constantly to dissolve the sugar, until the mixture just starts to simmer.
2. Remove from heat, transfer to a bowl, and cool to room temperature, letting the vanilla infuse in the sugar syrup. When the syrup is cool, remove the vanilla pod and discard.
3. Stir in the lemon zest, coffee, vodka, and Kahlua. Chill the mixture completely in the fridge.
4. Process the mixture in your ice cream maker according to the manufacturer's instructions. Transfer to a container. Freeze overnight.
5. Serve garnished with a couple of chocolate-covered espresso beans.

Sunny Amaretto Sorbet

MAKES ABOUT 1 QUART

3¼ cups freshly squeezed orange juice

½ cup sugar

½ cup fresh lemon juice

¼ cup Amaretto

Maraschino cherries, for garnish

This sunny take on the Amaretto Sour cocktail swaps in freshly squeezed orange juice for traditional, lemon-based sour mix. It's fruity, with hints of sweet almond. For a more traditional sour cocktail flavor, increase the amount of lemon juice, and decrease the orange juice.

1. Put the orange juice and sugar in a medium-sized pot. Simmer over medium-high heat until the sugar dissolves. Remove from heat. Cover and let cool to room temperature.
2. Stir in the lemon juice and Amaretto, then chill in the fridge until completely cold.
3. Process the mixture in your ice cream maker according to the manufacturer's instructions. Transfer to a container. Freeze overnight. Serve garnished with a few maraschino cherries.

Mix It In! Amaretto Sours are traditionally garnished with a maraschino cherry. Cherries and almonds are notoriously good companions. For a little more texture to this sorbet, try adding in ½ cup minced maraschino cherries in the last 5 minutes of processing.

Cognac & Apricot Sorbet

MAKES ABOUT 1 QUART

4 cups apricot nectar

½ cup fresh lemon juice

⅓ cup cognac

Cognac-soaked dried apricots, for garnish

Grab a bowl of this and settle in on the back porch after a leisurely Sunday brunch. It's packed with apricot flavor—with just a hint of cognac. Since bottled apricot nectar is already plenty sweet, any extra sugar has been omitted here.

1. Put the apricot nectar, lemon juice, and cognac in a medium-sized bowl. Whisk to combine. Chill in the fridge until completely cold.
2. Process the mixture in your ice cream maker according to the manufacturer's instructions. Transfer to a container. Freeze overnight.
3. Serve garnished with a single, luscious, cognac-soaked apricot.

> ## Cognac-Soaked Apricots
> **1 cup whole, dried apricots**
> **Cognac**
>
> Put the dried apricots in a clean mason jar. Cover with cognac. Cover and refrigerate for a week before serving. Use to garnish this sorbet, or any fruity cocktail. You can even chop up a handful and toss the pieces into cake batter or cookie dough for extra flavor.

Salty Dog Sorbet

MAKES ABOUT 1 QUART

4 cups grapefruit juice

1 cup sugar

¼ cup vodka

Pucker up! This frozen take on the classic Salty Dog cocktail is slightly tart and very refreshing. For a slightly sweeter sorbet, use ruby red grapefruit juice. To serve, scoop into goblets and garnish with a piece of candied grapefruit peel (or a wedge of gummy grapefruit, in a pinch) and a few flakes of sea salt.

1. Put the grapefruit juice and sugar in a medium-sized pot. Simmer over medium-high heat until the sugar dissolves. Remove from heat. Cover and let cool to room temperature.
2. Stir in the vodka, then chill in the fridge until completely cold.
3. Process the mixture in your ice cream maker according to the manufacturer's instructions. Transfer to a container. Freeze overnight.

Mexican Coffee Sorbet

MAKES ABOUT 1 QUART

¾ cup water

¾ cup dark brown sugar

3½ cups strong brewed coffee, chilled

¼ cup tequila

Whipped cream, for garnish

Cocoa powder, for garnish

Cayenne pepper, for garnish

If you like Mexican Coffee, that hot dessert coffee spiked with tequila, you'll love this sorbet. Serve with whipped cream dusted with cocoa powder and the tiniest bit of cayenne pepper.

1. Put the water, coffee, and brown sugar in a medium-sized pot. Cook over medium heat, whisking constantly to dissolve the sugar, until the mixture just starts to simmer.
2. Remove from heat, transfer to a bowl, and cool to room temperature. Stir in the tequila. Chill the mixture completely in the fridge.
3. Process the mixture in your ice cream maker according to the manufacturer's instructions. Transfer to a container. Freeze overnight.

Hurricane Sorbet

MAKES ABOUT 1 QUART

2 cups freshly squeezed orange juice

2 cups pineapple juice

¼ cup fresh lime juice

2 tablespoons light rum

2 tablespoons dark rum

2 tablespoons grenadine syrup

This sweet sorbet is a luscious mix of fruit juices liberally spiked with rum and a little grenadine syrup. It's a take on the classic Hurricane cocktail, invented in New Orleans in the '40s by bar owner Pat O'Brien.

1. Put all ingredients in a medium-sized bowl. Stir to combine. Chill in the fridge until completely cold.
2. Process the mixture in your ice cream maker according to the manufacturer's instructions. Transfer to a container. Freeze overnight.

Hurricane Dessert Cocktail

For a potent dessert cocktail, fill Hurricane glasses with 3 scoops of this sorbet. Add 1 shot of light rum and 1 shot of dark rum. Fill with equal parts chilled orange and pineapple juices. Garnish with a paper umbrella and a skewer of fresh pineapple chunks.

Orange Blossom Special Sorbet

MAKES ABOUT 1 QUART

3½ cups freshly squeezed orange juice

¾ cup sugar

Zest of 1 orange

1 tablespoon fresh lemon juice

¼ cup gin

The Orange Blossom cocktail is a heady mix of fresh orange juice and gin. This frozen version is bright and vibrant, with faint herbal notes from the gin.

1. Put the orange juice, sugar, and orange zest in a medium-sized pot. Simmer over medium-high heat until the sugar dissolves. Remove from heat. Cover and let cool to room temperature.
2. Stir in the lemon juice and gin, then chill in the fridge until completely cold.
3. Process the mixture in your ice cream maker according to the manufacturer's instructions. Transfer to a container. Freeze overnight.

Blueberry Mojito Sherbet

MAKES ABOUT 1 QUART

2 cups whole milk

4 cups blueberries

½ cup fresh mint leaves, roughly chopped

¾ cup sugar

Zest from 1 lime

¼ cup light rum

What a combination! This dramatically purple sherbet is packed with fresh blueberry juice. Mint accentuates the berry flavor.

1. Put the milk, blueberries, mint, sugar, and lime zest in your blender. Blend until smooth. Strain into a large bowl. Whisk in the light rum. Chill the mixture completely in the fridge.
2. Process the mixture in your ice cream maker according to the manufacturer's instructions. Transfer to a container. Freeze overnight.

> *Berry Substitutions* To change your berry flavor, substitute fresh raspberries, blackberries, or strawberries for the blueberries—or make a mixed berry mojito with any combination of these.

White Sangria Sorbet

MAKES ABOUT 1 QUART

1 cup orange juice

½ cup white grape juice

1½ cups sugar

1 cup strawberries, hulled and sliced

1 orange, sliced

1 lemon, sliced

3 cups pinot grigio

The nice thing about sangria is how versatile it is. You can make it with pretty much any fruit that's in season. This white sangria sorbet is light and citrusy, with just a hint of strawberry sweetness.

1. Put the orange juice, grape juice, and sugar in a medium-sized pot. Bring to a simmer, whisking until the sugar dissolves. Add the strawberries, sliced orange, and sliced lemon. Simmer over medium heat, stirring frequently, for about 10 minutes. Strain the mixture into a large bowl, smooshing the solids down with a spoon to extract as much liquid as you can. Discard the solids.
2. Add the pinot grigio, stirring to combine. Let cool to room temperature, then chill completely in the fridge.
3. Process the mixture in your ice cream maker according to the manufacturer's instructions. Transfer to a container. Freeze overnight.

Kiwi Cooler Sorbet

MAKES ABOUT 1 QUART

13 large, ripe kiwis

¾ cup sugar

1½ cups pinot grigio

This sorbet is a throwback to the early '90s, when you couldn't turn on the TV without seeing five or six wine cooler ads. Peeling all these kiwis is definitely a labor of love, but it's well worth the effort.

1. Peel, slice, and purée the kiwis in the blender. Add the sugar and pinot grigio. Purée until smooth. You want to wind up with about 2¼ cups of juice. Chill completely in the fridge.
2. Process the mixture in your ice cream maker according to the manufacturer's instructions. Transfer to a container. Freeze overnight.

Watermelon Margarita Sorbet

MAKES ABOUT 1 QUART

5-pound piece of ripe, seedless watermelon

½ cup sugar

Juice of 1 large lime

¼ cup tequila

Ever have a slice of spiked watermelon at a party? You know what I'm talking about: Punch a hole in a whole watermelon with a corkscrew, drain a small bottle of vodka or tequila into it, then slice it into delicious, semisolid cocktail wedges an hour or two later? This sorbet gets its inspiration from the very same cookout treat.

1. Chunk up the watermelon. Purée it in batches in the blender. You want to wind up with about 3½ cups of juice. (Getting juice out of whole fruit is an inexact science. The amount you get will vary slightly depending on how fleshy your watermelon is. When in doubt, buy a bigger piece of watermelon and deal with a little leftover.)
2. Add the sugar, lime juice, and tequila and blend until smooth. Give it a taste and add a little more sugar if it's too tart—or a little more lime juice if it's too sweet.
3. Chill completely in the fridge.
4. Process the mixture in your ice cream maker according to the manufacturer's instructions. Transfer to a container. Freeze overnight.

Chapter
9

Ice Cream Sandwiches, Cakes, and Other Frozen Novelties

Remember Carvel? Or your neighborhood ice cream truck? This section pays homage to those favorite frozen treats of our youth—the ice cream cakes, the pies, and the ice cream sandwiches.

You'll find frozen cheesecake recipes fit for royalty—without the need for a palatial kitchen. In fact, these scrumptious desserts take hardly any time, with none of the muss or fuss associated with traditional, baked cheesecakes.

For the ice cream pies, just grab a premade crust or follow my simple instructions and make your own buttery, cookie-based crust. The essence of these pies is really in the filling.

When it comes to ice cream sandwiches, use these recipes as a base, and get creative with your ice cream and cookie combinations. You can even make impromptu ice cream sandwiches with cookies from your local bakery—or your favorite homemade recipe.

Grand Marnier Frozen Cheesecake

MAKES 1 9-INCH CHEESECAKE

CRUST

1 cup graham cracker crumbs

2 tablespoons sugar

4 tablespoons butter, melted

FILLING

24 ounces cream cheese, at room temperature

½ cup sugar

½ cup heavy cream

½ cup marmalade

Zest from 1 orange

1 teaspoon vanilla extract

¼ cup Grand Marnier

Whipped cream and graham crackers, for garnish

Baked cheesecakes can be daunting to make, but this one is a real beauty. Since there's no baking, there's no cracking—and no real margin for messiness. Serve it as the finale at an intimate dinner party—or surprise your friends at your next movie night. Either way, this rich, marmalade-laced cheesecake is a real crowd pleaser.

1. Line the bottom of a 9" springform pan with a round of parchment paper.
2. Put the graham cracker crumbs in a bowl. Add the 2 tablespoons of sugar and the melted butter. Mix until uniform. Set aside.
3. To make the cheesecake, put the softened cream cheese, ½ cup of sugar, cream, marmalade, orange zest, vanilla extract, and Grand Marnier in the bowl of your stand mixer (or in a large bowl if using a handheld mixer). Beat on low until the mixture comes together. Then beat on medium-high for about 5 minutes, until the mixture is fluffy and uniform.
4. Transfer the mixture to your prepared pan. Smooth the surface down so it's relatively even. Sprinkle evenly with graham cracker mixture. Freeze overnight.
5. To serve, remove the outer ring of the springform pan and invert onto a serving plate. Slice with a sharp, unserrated knife. If you're having trouble, leave the cake on the counter for 20 minutes before slicing, or run your knife under hot water to warm it up.
6. Garnish with whipped cream and a small graham cracker.

> *Making Sure Cream Cheese is Room Temperature* Set the cream cheese out on the counter for half an hour to bring it up to room temperature before you use it. Be sure to make time to do this. If the cream cheese is too cold, it won't break up completely, and you'll wind up with little blobs in your finished cake.

Frozen Kahlua Cheesecake

MAKES 1 8-INCH CHEESECAKE

CRUST

1 cup chocolate graham cracker crumbs

2 tablespoons sugar

4 tablespoons butter, melted

½ cup mini chocolate chips

FILLING

24 ounces cream cheese, at room temperature

½ cup sugar

1 cup heavy cream

½ cup strong brewed coffee, chilled

1 teaspoon vanilla extract

¼ cup Kahlua

1 cup mini chocolate chips

Whipped cream, for garnish

Chocolate shavings, for garnish

It might sound dramatic, but chocolate graham crackers are a godsend. Bash them to bits and combine with a little butter, sugar, and chocolate, and they make the absolute best crust for any chocolate- or coffee-based frozen cheesecake or pie. (They also make killer s'mores.) The filling for this cheesecake is laced with coffee and Kahlua—and dotted with mini chocolate chips. Serve garnished with whipped cream and chocolate shavings.

1. Line the bottom of an 8" springform pan with a round of parchment paper.
2. Put the graham cracker crumbs in a bowl. Add the 2 tablespoons of sugar and the melted butter. Mix until uniform. Let cool completely. Mix in the mini chocolate chips. Set aside.
3. Make the cheesecake by putting the softened cream cheese, ½ cup of sugar, cream, brewed coffee, vanilla extract, and Kahlua in the bowl of your stand mixer (or in a large bowl if using a handheld mixer). Beat on low until the mixture comes together. Then beat on medium-high for about 5 minutes, until the mixture is fluffy and uniform. Fold in 1 cup of mini chocolate chips.
4. Transfer the mixture to your prepared pan. Smooth the surface down so it's relatively even. Sprinkle evenly with graham cracker mixture. Freeze overnight.
5. To serve, remove the outer ring of the springform pan and invert onto a serving plate. Slice with a sharp, unserrated knife. If you're having trouble, leave the cake on the counter for 20 minutes before slicing, or run your knife under hot water to warm it up.
6. Garnish with fresh whipped cream and chocolate shavings.

> *Graham Cracker Crumbs* Use packaged graham cracker crumbs (find them in the baking aisle of most big grocery stores) for this recipe—or make your own. To do this, put about 10–12 graham crackers in a zip-top bag. Seal and crush into crumbs with a rolling pin.

Frozen Chocolate Cream Pie

MAKES 1 9-INCH PIE

CRUST

3 cups Nabisco Famous Chocolate Wafers, crushed to crumbs

2 tablespoons sugar

5 tablespoons butter, melted

FILLING

2 cups heavy cream

1 cup whole milk

½ cup unsweetened cocoa powder

1 cup semisweet chocolate chips

6 egg yolks

¾ cup sugar

½ cup crème fraiche (or whole milk sour cream)

¼ cup chocolate liqueur

TOPPING

2 cups heavy cream

2 tablespoons sugar

1 tablespoon vanilla extract

Good-quality dark chocolate, shaved

Chocolate Cream Pie is one of those old-fashioned, grandmother desserts that's really hard to resist. This frozen version is made with crisp chocolate wafer cookies and a rich chocolate and crème fraiche ice cream. Top with fresh whipped cream and chocolate shavings right before serving for a stunning tableside presentation.

1. Make the crust by putting the chocolate cookie crumbs in a bowl. Add the 2 tablespoons of sugar and the melted butter. Mix until uniform. Let cool completely. To make the crust, press the crumbs into a 9" pie plate. Pop into the freezer to chill while you make the ice cream.
2. Make the ice cream by heating the cream and milk in a medium-sized, heavy-bottomed pot until the mixture just starts to steam. Remove from the heat and whisk in the cocoa powder and chocolate chips. Let it sit for 5 minutes, whisking occasionally, until the chocolate has melted and the mixture is uniform.
3. Put the egg yolks and ¾ cup sugar in a large bowl. Whisk until smooth.
4. Slowly ladle the chocolate mixture into the egg yolks, whisking constantly to combine. When you've added it all, transfer the mixture back to your pot.
5. Cook over medium heat, whisking constantly, until the mixture reaches 170°F on a candy thermometer. Don't let the mixture boil.
6. Strain the mixture into a large bowl to get rid of any tiny bits of cooked egg. Whisk in the crème fraiche and chocolate liqueur. Set the bowl in a larger bowl filled with ice, whisking frequently until the mixture cools to room temperature. Then refrigerate to chill completely, anywhere from 4–6 hours.
7. Process the mixture in your ice cream maker according to the manufacturer's instructions.
8. Assemble the pie by transferring the soft ice cream into your prepared pie crust. Smooth down the surface with a spatula. Freeze overnight.
9. Right before serving, make the topping. Put the cream, sugar, and vanilla extract in your mixer. Beat to stiff peaks. Heap on the pie. Top with chocolate shavings. Slice with a hot knife.

Frozen Key Lime Margarita Pie

MAKES 1 9-INCH PIE

CRUST

3 cups graham cracker crumbs

2 tablespoons sugar

5 tablespoons butter, melted

FILLING

16 ounces cream cheese, at room temperature

½ cup sugar

½ cup key lime juice

Zest of 1 lime

2 tablespoons tequila

Whipped cream, for garnish

Key Lime Pie is traditionally a mixture of sweetened condensed milk, egg yolks, and key lime juice. (See Chocolate Truffle Ice Cream recipe for more information on condensed milk.) This simplified version incorporates the same flavors in a cheesecake-type pie spiked with tequila. Fresh key limes can be hard to find, but bottled juice is readily available and perfectly acceptable for this pie.

1. Put the graham cracker crumbs in a bowl. Add the 2 tablespoons of sugar and the melted butter. Mix until uniform. Press into the pie plate to form your crust. Pop the pan into the freezer to chill while you make the filling.
2. Make the filling by microwaving the cream cheese for a minute or two to warm it up. This will make it much easier to stir.
3. Put the warm cream cheese, ½ cup of sugar, key lime juice, lime zest, and tequila in the bowl of your stand mixer (or in a large bowl if using a handheld mixer). Beat on low until the mixture comes together. Then beat on medium-high for about 5 minutes, until the mixture is fluffy and uniform.
4. Transfer the mixture to your prepared pan. Smooth the surface down so it's relatively even. Freeze overnight.
5. To serve, slice with a sharp, unserrated knife. If you're having trouble, leave the pie on the counter for 10 minutes before slicing, or run your knife under hot water to warm it up. Garnish with whipped cream.

The 2-Ingredient Sassy Vegan Banana

MAKES ABOUT 1 QUART

5 large ripe bananas, peeled and sliced into 1-inch chunks

¼ cup of crème de banana liqueur

This is a really great frozen dessert for folks who don't eat dairy. It's also really (like, really, really) easy—and makes for a practically instant dessert if you keep a bag of frozen, sliced bananas in your freezer. For the best flavor and consistency, make sure that your bananas are really ripe. You can also use it as a frozen pie filling as is. Just fill a 9-inch pie shell with it, smooth down, and freeze overnight.

1. Place the banana slices on a plate and freeze for about 2 hours.
2. Purée the frozen bananas and liqueur in your food processor or blender, stopping the machine as needed to scrape down the sides of the container and push the bananas down. (How much you have to monkey with it depends on how strong your processor or blender is.)
3. If they're not blending well, add a tablespoon or two of soy or almond milk to loosen the mixture up. Transfer to a container. Freeze overnight. Scoop into bowls and serve.
4. Customize your cocktail flavor! For a Vegan Banana Margarita, add ¼ cup tequila. For a Vegan Dirty Banana, add ¼ cup Kahlua. For a Vegan Bananas Foster, add ¼ cup dark rum.

Simple Fried Bananas

For an out-of-this-world sundae, garnish this recipe with hot, fried bananas.

1 large, ripe banana, peeled and sliced
1 tablespoon canola oil

Heat the canola oil in a nonstick pan over medium-high heat. Add the bananas, and cook until golden brown on the bottom, about 3 minutes. Flip and cook until golden brown on the bottom, another 3 minutes. Spoon over ice cream and serve immediately.

Molasses & Ginger Brandy Ice Cream Sandwiches

MAKES 12 ICE CREAM SANDWICHES

ICE CREAM

6 egg yolks

¾ cup sugar

1 tablespoon ground ginger

2 cups heavy cream

1 cup whole milk

¼ cup ginger brandy

½ cup candied ginger, finely chopped

COOKIES

8 tablespoons butter, softened

⅓ cup white sugar

⅓ cup brown sugar

½ teaspoon vanilla extract

1 jumbo egg

¼ cup molasses

1½ cups flour

½ teaspoon kosher salt

½ teaspoon baking powder

¼ teaspoon baking soda

1 tablespoon powdered ginger

½ teaspoon cinnamon

⅛ cup heavy cream

Here's a tasty little treat that's packed with ginger from start to finish. Make the ice cream and bake the cookies one day, then assemble the sandwiches the next day. The ice cream needs to set up overnight. For extra oomph, roll the sandwiches in finely chopped candied ginger.

TO MAKE THE ICE CREAM

1. Whisk the egg yolks, sugar, and ground ginger together in a large bowl until light and fluffy. Set aside.
2. Put the milk and cream in a medium-sized, heavy-bottomed pot. Cook over medium heat, whisking occasionally, until the mixture just starts to simmer around the edges.
3. Remove the pot from the heat. Slowly drizzle the hot mixture into the egg yolk mixture, whisking constantly to temper it. Return the combined mixture to the pot. Cook over medium heat, whisking constantly, until it registers 170°F on a candy thermometer and is thick enough to coat the back of a spoon.
4. Remove from the heat. Strain the mixture into a large bowl. Stir in the ginger brandy. Cool in an ice bath, then refrigerate until totally chilled, about 4–6 hours. Process in your ice cream maker according to the manufacturer's instructions, adding the chopped candied ginger in the last 5 minutes. Transfer to a container and freeze overnight until solid.

TO BAKE THE COOKIES

1. Preheat your oven to 375°F. Line two sheet pans with parchment paper and set aside.
2. Beat the softened butter, white sugar, and brown sugar in your mixer until light and fluffy. Add the egg, vanilla extract, and molasses and beat until uniform.
3. In a separate bowl, whisk together the flour, salt, baking powder, baking soda, powdered ginger, and cinnamon.

4. Beat half of the dry ingredients into the wet ingredients. Add the cream and beat to incorporate. Beat in the rest of the dry ingredients until the dough is uniform. It should be the consistency of thick peanut butter.

5. Using a small soup spoon, drop the dough onto your prepared sheet pans. You want to wind up with 24 evenly sized blobs of dough. Bake for about 10 minutes, until they're barely brown on the bottom and edges. Cool on a wire rack.

6. Assemble the ice cream sandwiches: Line a sheet pan with parchment paper. Let the ice cream stand on the counter for about 20 minutes to soften up.

7. Put a scoop or two of ice cream on one cookie. Top with another cookie and gently press it down so the ice cream spreads to the edges. Set on your prepared sheet pan. Repeat with the rest of the cookies.

8. Pop the pan into the freezer for about an hour so the ice cream firms back up. Wrap each sandwich in waxed paper. Return to the freezer and freeze for 3–6 hours, until solid.

Frozen Peanut Butter Cups with Castries Crème Liqueur

MAKES ABOUT 2 DOZEN MINI PEANUT BUTTER CUPS

FILLING

1¼ cups smooth peanut butter

½ cup powdered sugar

1 teaspoon vanilla extract

¼ cup Castries Crème Liqueur

CHOCOLATE SHELLS

3–4 cups semisweet chocolate chips

24 paper mini-muffin liners

Castries Crème Liqueur is an intoxicating blend of rum, cream, and peanuts made in tropical St. Lucia. It easily takes these peanut butter cups from really good to straight up out of this world. Definitely take the time to find a bottle if you can. In a pinch, substitute an equal amount of dark rum.

1. Start by making the filling. Put the peanut butter, powdered sugar, vanilla extract, and Castries Crème Liqueur in a bowl. Stir until uniform. Set aside.
2. Make the chocolate shells by melting the chocolate chips in a double boiler or the microwave. Let the chocolate cool on the counter until it's cool enough to handle comfortably.
3. Put a small spoonful of melted chocolate in a paper muffin liner. Spread it all over the inside of the liner with the back of the spoon. Set the coated liner aside on a large plate. Repeat with the rest of the liners.
4. Reserve the remaining melted chocolate.
5. Pop the plate with the liners into the fridge until the chocolate has hardened, about an hour. When the shells are hard, fill each about three-quarters to the top with peanut butter filling. Smush the filling down so it's relatively flat.
6. Top each with a spoonful of the reserved melted chocolate. Spread the chocolate to the edges, so that it completely covers the filling. Using the back of a spoon, swirl the top of the chocolate for a nice presentation.
7. Set each finished peanut butter cup on a freezer-safe tray. Repeat with the rest of the chocolate shells.
8. Freeze overnight on the tray. If you need to store them longer, once they're frozen solid, wrap each in waxed paper and store in a zip-top bag in the freezer for up to a month.

Hot Buttered Rum Pecan Sundae

MAKES 1–2 SERVINGS

2 tablespoons butter

3 tablespoons brown sugar

½ cup pecan halves

¼ cup dark rum

Vanilla ice cream

This is a casual, quick, totally decadent sundae. The candied pecans are robed in a thick, fragrant, brown sugar–rum sauce. Fill your bowl with as much vanilla ice cream as you like. This is delicious with the Spice Trader's Vanilla Vodka Ice Cream in Chapter 3.

1. Melt the butter on the stove in a nonstick pan over medium heat. Add the brown sugar. Stir to combine. Cook for a minute or two over medium heat, stirring constantly.
2. Toss the pecans into the pan. Stir to coat. Cook for another minute or two over medium heat, stirring constantly.
3. Take the pan off the heat. Add the rum. Be careful—it will immediately start to boil and let off a big poof of steam. Stir to incorporate the rum into the sauce.
4. Return the pan to the stove over low heat. Cook for another minute, stirring constantly, until the nuts are coated and the sauce is thick and glossy.
5. Take the pan off the heat. Scoop a bowlful of vanilla ice cream. Top with candied pecans and sauce. Serve immediately.

Kirsch Bombe

MAKES 6–8 SERVINGS

1 quart Cherry Bomb Ice Cream
(see Chapter 3), softened

4–5 cups fresh cherries, stemmed,
pitted, and sliced

1 pint vanilla ice cream, softened

Whipped cream, for garnish

A bombe is an impressive, layered and molded French ice cream dessert. This one is deceptively easy to make, with layers of cherry and vanilla ice cream separated by sliced, sweet cherries. A set of freezer-safe nesting bowls makes this a snap. You can find them at most big home goods stores.

1. Put an 8-inch bowl in the freezer. When it's cold, line it with some of the softened Cherry Bomb ice cream, reserving the rest. Gently press a layer of fresh cherries onto the cherry ice cream. Set a layer of plastic wrap on top of the cherries. Set a 6-inch bowl on top of the cherries. Press the bowl down gently so it evens the ice cream out and keeps it in place. Freeze until solid, about an hour.

2. Remove the 6-inch bowl. Add a layer of softened vanilla ice cream on top of the frozen cherries. Gently press a layer of fresh cherries onto the vanilla ice cream. Set a layer of plastic wrap on top of the cherries. Set a 4-inch bowl on top of the cherries. Press it down gently so it evens the ice cream out and keeps it in place. Freeze until solid.

3. Remove the 4-inch bowl. Fill the center of the bombe with softened Cherry Bomb Ice Cream. Cover the surface of the ice cream with plastic wrap. Freeze until solid.

4. To serve, dip the bowl in a larger bowl of warm water. Set a flat plate on top of the ice cream and invert the bowl to unmold the bombe. Slice with a hot, sharp knife.

Amaretto Ice Cream Sandwiches

**MAKES 12 ICE CREAM
SANDWICHES**

FOR 24 COOKIES

1½ cups flour

½ teaspoon baking soda

¾ teaspoon salt

1 cup brown sugar, firmly packed

8 tablespoons butter, softened

1 egg

2 teaspoons almond extract

1 quart Toasted Amaretto Gelato
(see Chapter 4)

Sliced almonds, toasted

The only thing that could make almond ice cream better is to wedge it between a couple of almond-scented butter cookies. That's just what these sandwiches do. To up the almond ante, they're also rolled in toasted, sliced almonds.

1. Start by making the cookies. Whisk the flour, baking soda, and salt together in a medium-sized bowl. Set aside.
2. In the bowl of your stand mixer or a large bowl if using a handheld mixer, beat the brown sugar and butter together until well combined. Add the egg and almond extract. Beat until light and fluffy.
3. Add in the flour mixture. Beat quickly to combine well. Stop mixing when the dough just comes together. (Overmixing can make the cookies tough.)
4. Spoon the dough out into the center of a large piece of wax paper. With your hands, form it into a log that's about 2½ inches in diameter, give or take.
5. Wrap the paper around the dough tightly and roll it up like a burrito. Twist the ends tightly. Pop it into the fridge for a few hours to firm up the dough.
6. Preheat your oven to 350°F. Line two sheet pans with parchment paper and set aside. Slice the cookie dough into 24 even slices. Space the slices out on your prepared pans.
7. Bake at 350°F for about 10 minutes, until just golden brown. Cool on a wire rack.
8. Let the Toasted Amaretto Gelato stand on the counter for about 20 minutes to soften up. Line a sheet pan with parchment paper.
9. Assemble the ice cream sandwiches: Put a scoop or two of gelato on one cookie. Top with another cookie and gently press it down so the gelato spreads to the edges.
10. Roll in sliced, toasted almonds to coat the edges. Set on your prepared sheet pan. Repeat with the rest of the cookies.
11. Pop the pan into the freezer for about an hour so the gelato firms back up. Wrap each sandwich in waxed paper. Return to the freezer and freeze for 3–6 hours, until solid.

Mini Mint Chocolate Chip Sandwiches

MAKES 12–16

1 quart Grasshopper Gelato (see Chapter 4)

24–28 soft chocolate chip cookies, baked and cooled

Dark chocolate chips

Bake your favorite chocolate chip cookies—or get a couple dozen soft chocolate chip cookies at your local bakery. These are just the right size for a quick snack. For a dramatic presentation at your next party, double or triple the recipe and serve heaped on a platter. Put the dark chocolate chips in a wide, shallow bowl and set aside.

1. Line a sheet pan with parchment paper. Put the dark chocolate chips in a wide, shallow bowl and set aside. Let the Grasshopper Gelato stand on the counter for about 20 minutes to soften up.
2. Put a scoop or two of gelato on one cookie. Top with another cookie and gently press it down so the gelato spreads to the edges. Roll the sandwiches in the bowl of dark chocolate chips until the edges are coated. Set on your prepared sheet pan. Repeat with the rest of the cookies.
3. Pop the pan into the freezer for about an hour so the gelato firms up. Wrap each sandwich in waxed paper. Return to the freezer and freeze for 3–6 hours, until solid.

Chapter
10

Frozen Cocktails, Milkshakes, and Smoothies

Give almost anyone the choice between dessert and a cocktail after dinner, and chances are they'll pick dessert. These concoctions easily serve as both.

All you need is a well-stocked bar, a bag of ice, and a decent blender to crush it. And it doesn't have to cost a fortune. If you want to try a drink that includes a pricey liquor, just grab a few nips or a pint at the liquor store. That way, you can experiment without a huge expense.

Frozen Zombie

SERVES 1 GENEROUSLY

1½ cups ice

1½ ounces dark rum

1 ounce light rum

½ ounce 151-proof rum

½ ounce cherry liqueur

1¼ ounces fresh lemon juice

¾ ounce fresh orange juice

2 dashes grenadine syrup

Maraschino cherries and fresh orange slices, for garnish

There's a zombie and brain freeze joke here that's just itching to be told, but I'll spare you. If you've ever been to a tiki bar, you're probably familiar with the Zombie cocktail. It's the drink that most bartenders limit to two per patron because it's so darned strong. This frozen version is no exception. It packs a fruity, frosty punch.

1. Put the ice in your blender. Add all the ingredients. Blend until smooth. Pour into a glass.
2. Garnish with a skewer of alternating maraschino cherries and fresh orange slices.

Frozen Gin Fizz

SERVES 1

1 cup ice

3 ounces gin

Juice of half a lemon

1½ teaspoons powdered sugar

Soda water or lemon-lime soda

Lemon or lime slice, for garnish

In order to be a fizz, a cocktail needs to have soda water and either lemon or lime juice. This frozen cocktail has both the soda and the juice—and a generous amount of gin. It makes a great summertime cooler.

1. Put the ice in your blender. Add the gin, lemon juice, and powdered sugar. Blend until smooth. Pour into a glass. Top with soda water (or a splash of lemon-lime soda, for a sweeter twist).
2. Garnish with a slice of lemon or lime.

Arctic Scorpion Bowl

SERVES 4

2 cups ice

2 ounces gin

1 ounce dark rum

2 ounces 151-proof rum

2 ounces light rum

2 ounces vodka

2 ounces grenadine syrup

4 ounces freshly squeezed orange juice

4 ounces pineapple juice

Orange slices, pineapple chunks, and maraschino cherries, for garnish

The Scorpion Bowl is something of a legend at our house. It's a must for almost all celebrations with close friends. This drink serves four generously. For true tiki style, serve it in a bowl with four straws.

1. Fill your blender with ice. Add all ingredients. Blend until smooth.
2. Garnish with a skewer of orange slices, pineapple chunks, and maraschino cherries.

Frozen Mint Julep

SERVES 1

1 cup ice

2 ounces bourbon

1 ounce lemon juice

1 ounce simple syrup

1 sprig of mint + more for garnish

Get in that Kentucky Derby spirit anytime with this Frozen Mint Julep. This minty, bourbon-soaked drink is traditionally served in a silver or pewter cup—or more popularly in a Collins glass.

1. Put the ice in your blender. Add the bourbon, lemon juice, simple syrup, and one sprig of mint. Blend until smooth.
2. Pour and garnish with additional fresh mint.

Raging Frozen Aztec

SERVES 2

1 cup ice

2 ounces Bailey's Irish Cream

2 ounces Kahlua

2 ounces vodka

1 tablespoon hot fudge sauce

1/8 teaspoon ground cayenne pepper

1 cup chocolate milk

Marshmallow fluff, for garnish

Unsweetened cocoa powder, for garnish

Aztec hot chocolate, also known as cocoa that's been spiked with a little chili pepper, is the perfect winter drink. This potent frozen version is great year-round.

1. Put the ice in your blender. Add the Bailey's Irish Cream, Kahlua, vodka, hot fudge sauce, ground cayenne pepper, and chocolate milk. Blend until smooth.
2. To serve, pour into a glass. Top with a dollop of marshmallow fluff and dust with cocoa powder.

> *Quick Tip* For less heat, use a milder chili pepper, like ancho or poblano.

Frozen Cosmo

SERVES 1

1 cup ice

1/2 ounce triple sec

2 ounces vodka

3–4 ounces cranberry juice

Lime wedge, for garnish

Cosmos never go out of style. Serve them frozen for a crisp, refreshing summer drink.

1. Put the ice in your blender.
2. Add the triple sec, vodka, and cranberry juice.
3. Blend until smooth.
4. Pour and garnish with a lime wedge.

Drunken Penguin

SERVES 1

1 cup ice

1 ounce gin

1 ounce dry vermouth

½ teaspoon maraschino liqueur

½ teaspoon absinthe

3 dashes orange bitters

Maraschino cherry and lemon twist, for garnish

This is a frozen take on the classic Tuxedo cocktail, from the *Harry Johnson Bartenders' Manual* of 1882.

1. Put the ice in your blender.
2. Add the gin, dry vermouth, maraschino liqueur, absinthe, and orange bitters.
3. Blend until smooth.
4. Pour into a glass.
5. Top with a cherry and hang a lemon twist off the glass.

St. Germaine Frozen Punch

SERVES 6+

Ice

1 (750-ml) bottle pinot grigio, chilled

4 ounces St. Germaine elderflower liqueur

4 ounces vodka

3–5 fresh mint leaves + sprigs for garnish

Ginger ale

St. Germaine is a sweet, elderflower liqueur that pairs beautifully with light-bodied white wines. Fresh mint is a great counterpoint to the fragrant liqueur.

1. Fill your blender halfway with ice. Purée half the wine, St. Germaine, vodka, and mint. Blend until smooth, adding more wine until you've achieved a smoothie consistency.
2. Pour into tall glasses. Top with a splash of ginger ale. Garnish with mint sprigs.

Maple Bourbon Sugar Shack Shake

SERVES 1–2 GENEROUSLY

4 cups vanilla ice cream

1 cup whole milk

¼ cup maple syrup

¼ cup bourbon

Maple sugar candy, for garnish

The combination of maple syrup and vanilla ice cream in this shake is just screaming for a little bourbon. The result is intoxicatingly delicious. Be sure to use real maple syrup for this one, not artificially flavored pancake syrup.

1. Put all ingredients in your blender and blend until smooth. Pour into a tall glass.
2. To garnish, wedge a piece of maple sugar candy on the rim.

Black Raspberry & Chambord Frappe

SERVES 1–2 GENEROUSLY

3 cups black raspberry ice cream

1 cup frozen raspberries

1 cup whole milk

¼ cup Chambord

2 tablespoons vodka

Fresh raspberries, for garnish

Talk about purple passion. This deep, berry-colored frappe gets its flavor from black raspberry ice cream, frozen raspberries (which stand in nicely for ice), and Chambord.

1. Put all ingredients in your blender and blend until smooth.
2. Pour into a tall glass.
3. Garnish with a skewer of fresh raspberries.

> *What the Heck Is a Frappe?* Frappe is a New England term for a milkshake that may or may not be made with a little ice. Whatever you call it, it's downright delicious.

Smooth Dark & Stormy

SERVES 1

3 cups ginger ice cream

½ cup candied ginger, chopped

1 cup whole milk

¼ cup dark rum

Candied ginger, for garnish

Dark & Stormies, made with dark rum and ginger beer are a perfect spicy autumn drink. Here's a frozen version of the cocktail, in creamy milkshake form.

1. Put the ginger ice cream, ½ cup chopped candied ginger, milk, and dark rum in your blender and blend until smooth.
2. Pour into a pint glass.
3. Garnish with candied ginger.

> *Substitutions* If you can't find ginger ice cream, substitute good vanilla ice cream and use 2 tablespoons of dark rum and 2 tablespoons of ginger liquor.

Cookies & Irish Cream Milkshake

SERVES 2

3 cups vanilla ice cream

1 cup whole milk

2 ounces Bailey's Irish Cream

2 ounces chocolate liqueur

3 Oreo cookies, plus 1 more for garnish

There's something totally delightful about throwing a couple of Oreos into the blender. This Cookies & Cream milkshake gets its kick from some chocolate liqueur and a little Bailey's Irish Cream.

1. Put the vanilla ice cream, milk, Bailey's, chocolate liqueur, and 3 Oreos in the blender.
2. Blend until smooth.
3. Pour into a pint glass.
4. Garnish with an Oreo cookie.

> *Oreo Garnish* Here's an easy way to make an Oreo sit politely on the rim of your glass. Carefully twist the cookie apart. Scrape all the cream over to one side. Stick the cookie back together on the rim of your glass, with the cream holding the two sides together at the top.

Guinness Float

SERVES 1

1 can of Guinness

3 scoops vanilla ice cream

If you've never thought of combining stout with ice cream, you don't know what you're missing. Rich vanilla ice cream is the perfect companion for creamy, smooth Guinness. If you haven't had one, you're in for a treat.

1. Scoop the vanilla ice cream into a pint glass.
2. Pour in the Guinness bit by bit, letting the head subside a little in between pours.
3. Add a straw and a long spoon to your glass, and go to town! Cheers!

Woodchuck Apple Cider Slider

SERVES 1

3 cups vanilla ice cream

⅛ teaspoon ground cinnamon

½ cup unfiltered apple cider

½ cup Woodchuck hard cider

Whipped cream and ground cinnamon, for garnish

This slider is like apple pie in a glass. It combines classic mouthwatering, autumn flavors in one smooth, creamy shake with just a hint of fizz.

1. Put the vanilla ice cream, ground cinnamon, and unfiltered apple cider in your blender and blend until smooth.
2. Pour into a tall glass.
3. Stir in the hard cider.
4. Garnish with whipped cream and a dusting of ground cinnamon.

Frozen Long Island Iced Tea

SERVES 2

2 cups ice

1½ cups sour mix

1 ounce vodka

1 ounce gin

1 ounce light rum

1 ounce tequila

1 ounce triple sec

Cola

Fresh orange slices

Maraschino cherries

Watch out: This is a strong one. Long Island Iced Tea is a super-charged combination of five liquors topped with a splash of cola. Try to limit your guests to two each. They're potent—and really easy to drink, especially on a hot summer day.

1. Put the ice, sour mix, vodka, gin, light rum, tequila, and triple sec in the blender.
2. Blend until uniform.
3. Pour into two tall glasses.
4. Top with a splash of cola.
5. Garnish with a skewer of orange slices and maraschino cherries.
6. Serve immediately.

Chapter 11

Toppings and Treats

Last but certainly not least, these embellishments, sauces, and toppings will help you make your frozen treats extraordinary.

Ever had a homemade marshmallow? Mmmmmm! This chapter includes recipes for homemade candies, which are great drink additions—and serve as perfectly delicious treats in their own right.

How about yummy sauces? Most of the major ice cream toppings are included here—butterscotch, marshmallow sauce, and hot fudge. You'll even find homemade maraschino cherries to top things off!

Dulce de Leche

MAKES ABOUT 1 CUP

1 quart whole milk

1½ cups sugar

1 vanilla bean

½ teaspoon baking soda

Dulce de leche is a popular Latin American sweet that translates roughly into something like milk jam or milk candy. This caramel spread is made by reducing milk, sugar, and vanilla until the concoction is so thick you can stand a spoon up in it. You can buy perfectly acceptable dulce de leche in stores, but if you have about three hours, it's well worth the effort to make it at home. Use the best whole milk you can find. It's absolutely outstanding. Drizzle dulce de leche on top of sundaes, or swirl it into ice cream or brownie batter. Use it anywhere you want a kiss of deep caramel flavor.

1. Put the milk and sugar in a medium-sized, heavy-bottomed pot. Whisk to combine. Slit your vanilla bean in half lengthwise with a sharp knife. With the back of your knife, scrape out the paste. Toss the vanilla paste and pod into the pot with the milk.
2. Cook over medium heat, whisking frequently, until the sugar dissolves. Whisk in the baking soda.
3. Cook until the mixture just starts to bubble at the edges, then knock the heat down to low, so that it barely holds a simmer. Cook like this, uncovered, stirring occasionally for about 1 hour. (Warning: If your heat is too high, the milk can start to boil rapidly, which means that it can bubble up and possibly over onto your stove. Keep an eye on the pot until you're sure that the heat is right.)
4. As it cooks, it will start to slowly turn a lovely golden color. After 1 hour, remove the vanilla pod and discard. Continue to cook on low heat for another 1½ to 2 hours, stirring occasionally.
5. It's done when it's thick, sticky, and nut brown in color. Take the pot off the heat. Strain into a medium-sized bowl. Cool to room temperature on the counter, then pop it into the fridge to chill completely. It will keep for about a month.

Homemade Marshmallows

MAKES ABOUT 1½ POUNDS OF MARSHMALLOWS

5 tablespoons unflavored gelatin

2 cups cold water, divided

3 cups sugar

2 cups light corn syrup

½ teaspoon salt

4 tablespoons vanilla extract

Powdered sugar, for dusting

Once you've had a homemade marshmallow, you'll never go back to store bought. They're that good. This is a big recipe. Making marshmallows is a fun, sticky project, so I tend to like to make a lot at once. They keep for a few months, and make great gifts. If they last that long, that is.

1. Put the gelatin and 1 cup of cold water in the bowl of your mixer. Stir to combine. Let it sit uncovered for about 30 minutes, until solid.
2. With a strainer, dust a 9 × 13 glass baking dish with a thick layer of powdered sugar.
3. Make the sugar syrup by putting 1 cup of water, the sugar, salt, and corn syrup in a deep, medium-sized pot on the stove over high heat. Whisk until uniform.
4. As the mixture comes to a boil, wash down the sides of the pot with a brush dipped in cold water. Boil the sugar (keep the heat on high) until it reaches 244°F on a candy thermometer. Remove the pot from the heat.
5. With the mixer running on low, slowly and carefully pour the hot sugar mixture into the gelatin. At this point, it's going to smell kind of awful. (Unflavored gelatin is stinky business.) Trust me and don't worry about it. You'll fix it with a little vanilla extract at the end.
6. Beat the mixture on medium-high for about 20 minutes, until the mixture has turned into thick, opaque white marshmallow fluff. Beat in the vanilla extract. Give the mixture a taste. It should taste like heavenly, sweet marshmallow.
7. Pour the marshmallow fluff slowly into your prepared pans. Dust the tops of the marshmallow with more powdered sugar. Leave the pans uncovered on the counter overnight to set up.
8. To cut the marshmallows, put a cup or two of powdered sugar in a gallon-size zip-top bag. Dip a thin, sharp knife in a glass of hot water, then run the knife around the inside edge of each pan until the marshmallow loosens. Lift the entire piece out and set it on a board. Cut into squares, tossing each one in the bag and rolling it in powdered sugar to completely coat. Repeat until you've cut all your marshmallows.

Homemade Vanilla Extract

2–3 whole vanilla beans

1–2 cups good-quality vodka

1 glass bottle with cap

This is arguably the best vanilla vodka that you'll ever have. Here's the catch: It takes a while to make. Vanilla extract is basically an infusion, so you have to be patient as your vanilla beans give up all their lovely flavor. Be sure to use good-quality vodka that you wouldn't mind drinking. Make a few extra bottles and give them to your favorite bakers around the holidays.

1. Sterilize your bottle and cap by washing with hot, soapy water. Let it dry thoroughly.
2. Pop the vanilla beans into the bottle. Fill with vodka. Cap the bottle. Let it sit in your kitchen in a cool, dark place for 6–8 weeks. Shake occasionally.
3. Want to speed up the process a little? Use more beans and a bit less vodka.

Never-ending Extract Once you've made a bottle of vanilla extract, keep it going. As you use it, replenish it with more vodka and vanilla beans. My homemade vanilla extract lives in an old-fashioned glass milk bottle. I've had it going since 2002. It must have two dozen vanilla beans in it—and it has far and away better flavor than anything I can find in a store.

Hot Fudge Sauce

MAKES ABOUT 3 CUPS

¾ cup unsweetened cocoa powder

⅔ cup whole milk

7 tablespoons butter

2 cups sugar

4 tablespoons light corn syrup

2 teaspoons vanilla extract

2 tablespoons crème de cacao

Homemade hot fudge is really simple to make—and is so much better than anything you can buy in a jar. Use the best cocoa powder you can get your paws on.

1. Put the cocoa powder, milk, butter, sugar, and corn syrup on the stove in a small pot over medium heat. Stir constantly. It will be lumpy and messy until it heats up and the ingredients melt together into a smooth mixture.

2. Bring the mixture up to a simmer. As it heats up, wash down the sides of the pot with a brush dipped in cold water. This is important, as it'll keep rogue sugar crystals from invading your hot fudge and crystallizing in the fridge. Simmer for about 5 minutes.

3. Remove the pan from the heat. Stir in the vanilla extract and crème de cacao. Transfer to a bowl. Cool to room temperature, then cover and refrigerate. This will keep in the refrigerator for about a month.

Oh, Fudge! My Sauce Is Solid! If your sauce is too firm once it's cold, simply pop it in the microwave for a few seconds to warm it up.

Candied Orange Peel

MAKES ABOUT ¾–1 POUND CANDY, DEPENDING ON HOW BIG YOUR ORANGES ARE

3–4 large oranges

4 cups water

5 cups sugar, divided

Use this basic technique to candy any kind of citrus peel—lemon, lime, grapefruit, blood orange, you name it. Candied peel will keep for about two months tightly wrapped in plastic wrap in the fridge.

1. If possible, choose fruit that hasn't been sprayed or treated. Rinse your fruit under cold water and wipe it down.
2. With a sharp paring knife, cut the peel off the orange in wide strips. Get as much of the colored peel as you can—and as little of the soft white pith beneath it, which is very bitter. Once you've removed the peel, slice it into thin strips. I like to go about pencil width.
3. Blanch the peels by bringing a few inches of water to boil on the stove in a medium-sized pot. Drop in the strips of orange peel. Give them a stir. Boil for about 20 minutes to remove any bitterness. Drain in a colander.
4. Put 4 cups of water and 4 cups of sugar in a large pot. Whisk to combine. Bring to a boil, whisking until the sugar melts. Toss in the boiled orange peels. Give a stir. Knock the heat down a little, so that the sugar syrup holds a simmer. Simmer the peels, uncovered, for about 45 minutes, until translucent.
5. Line a baking sheet with paper towels. Set a wire rack on top of the towels. Fish the peels out of the syrup with a fork. Set them on your prepared rack to drain for about 15 minutes.
6. Put 1 cup of sugar in a medium-sized bowl. Drop a few pieces of the peel into the sugar. Toss to coat. Set them on a clean wire rack. Repeat with the rest of the peels. Let them air dry overnight. Transfer to an airtight container.

Marshmallow Sauce

MAKES ABOUT 2 CUPS

4 large egg whites

½ teaspoon cream of tartar

1½ cups light corn syrup

1 cup sugar

½ cup water

1 tablespoon vanilla extract

On the marshmallow continuum, this sauce is somewhere in between soft, pillow-y marshmallows and thick, sticky fluff. Use it to top sundaes—or swirl it through ice cream or gelato right before you pop it into the freezer.

1. Put the egg whites and cream of tartar in the bowl of your stand mixer and beat to stiff peaks. Set aside.

2. Whisk the corn syrup, sugar and water together in a small, heavy-bottomed pot. Set on the stove over high heat. Bring to a boil. Boil, without stirring, until the mixture is a light caramel color and registers 240°F on a candy thermometer. Remove the pot from the heat.

3. With your stand mixer running on low, slowly pour the hot syrup into the beaten egg whites. (Be really careful! Hot sugar is like napalm.) Beat until fluffy and opaque, about 3 minutes. Beat in the vanilla extract.

4. Transfer the sauce to a bowl. Cover and refrigerate before using. This will keep for about a month in the refrigerator.

Butterscotch Sauce

MAKES ABOUT 2 CUPS

8 tablespoons butter

2 cups dark brown sugar

1½ cups heavy cream

2 teaspoons kosher salt

2 tablespoons vanilla extract

This sauce has a richer, more buttery taste than a traditional caramel or dulce de leche. Don't skimp on the salt—it's what helps balance out the flavor.

1. Melt the butter in a medium-sized, heavy-bottomed pot over medium heat on the stove. Stir in the brown sugar. Cook for a few minutes until the sugar melts, stirring frequently.
2. Add the cream. Whisk to combine. Simmer over medium heat for about 7 minutes, whisking constantly.
3. Remove the pot from the heat. Whisk in the salt and vanilla extract. Transfer to a bowl. Let cool to room temperature. Cover and refrigerate. This will keep for about a month in the refrigerator.

Crème Chantilly

MAKES ABOUT 1½ CUPS

2 tablespoons sugar

1 cup whipping cream

¼ teaspoon vanilla extract

Crème Chantilly is Plain Jane Whipped Cream's sophisticated older sister. It's sweet and fragrant with vanilla. In terms of a garnish, a dollop of Crème Chantilly is the perfect canvas for a dusting of just about anything—ground cinnamon, chocolate shavings, lemon zest. Use your imagination!

1. Put the sugar, cream, and vanilla extract in a large bowl.
2. Beat to soft peaks. (Depending on what you're garnishing, if you need a sturdier cream, beat to stiff peaks.)

Orange Melba Sauce

MAKES ABOUT 2 CUPS

24 ounces fresh raspberries

1 cup freshly squeezed orange juice

1 cup sugar

Classic Melba sauce is an exquisite raspberry sauce that famed French chef Auguste Escoffier whipped up for his favorite opera singer, Dame Nellie Melba. This thick, glossy red sauce is delicious drizzled over ice cream and frozen cheesecake. Add a hint of orange and it's even better. You can also use it as a flavor base for cocktails and adult smoothies.

1. Put the raspberries, orange juice, and sugar in a medium-sized, heavy-bottomed pot. Stir to combine. Bring to a boil over medium-high heat, stirring occasionally.

2. When the mixture boils, stir it constantly, mashing the berries against the side of the pot to break them up. Boil for about 3 minutes, until the mixture is syrupy and coats the back of a spoon thickly.

3. Remove the pot from the heat. Give the sauce a taste. If it's too sweet for your liking, add a little more orange juice (or even a little lemon juice), then cook until thick again.

4. Strain the sauce into a bowl, stirring the mixture in the strainer to help push the liquid through. Cool the sauce to room temperature, then cover and refrigerate. It will thicken a little as it cools. This sauce will keep for about 4 days in the fridge.

A Few Flavor Twists Try adding a little fresh thyme, basil, or rosemary to the pot at the beginning. All these herbs get along famously with raspberries.

Spiced Candied Nuts

MAKES ABOUT 2 CUPS

1 cup sugar

¼ teaspoon ground cinnamon

¼ teaspoon ground cloves

3 cups shelled, unsalted nuts

This is a really fast way to make candied nuts. Use any kind of unsalted nuts you like. Swap in your favorite spices. Candied cashews with cardamom are to die for.

1. Line a sheet pan with parchment paper. Set aside.
2. Combine the sugar, cinnamon, and ground cloves in a heavy-bottomed, medium pot over medium heat. Cook like this, whisking constantly, until the sugar is caramel colored and smells amazing.
3. Remove the pot from the heat. Immediately toss the nuts into the pot, stirring with a spoon to coat them evenly.
4. When they're coated, pour them onto your prepared pan, and spread them out so they're not touching. (If they're touching, they'll stick together when the sugar hardens.) Move like lightning. The sugar hardens really quickly.
5. Let cool completely. Transfer to an airtight container. Candied nuts will keep for about 2 weeks on the counter.

Boozy Bourbon Brown Sugar Sauce

MAKES 2 CUPS

6 egg yolks

¾ cup dark brown sugar

2 cups heavy cream

1 whole vanilla bean

½ cup bourbon

This warm bourbon sauce is thick, rich, and flecked with vanilla. Serve it instead of hot fudge over ice cream. It also makes a killer sauce for buttery, homemade pound cake.

1. Whisk the egg yolks and brown sugar together in a large bowl. Set aside.
2. Put the cream in a medium-sized, heavy-bottomed pot. Slit the vanilla bean in half lengthwise with a sharp knife. Scrape out the paste with the back of your knife. Add the vanilla pod and paste to the pot. Cook the mixture over medium heat, whisking occasionally, until the mixture just starts to bubble at the edges.
3. Remove the pot from the heat. Let stand for about 15 minutes to infuse. Remove the vanilla pod and discard.
4. Slowly drizzle the hot mixture into the beaten egg mixture, whisking constantly. Return the combined mixture to the pot. Cook over medium heat, whisking constantly, for 4–5 minutes, until it thickens and registers 160°F on a candy thermometer.
5. Remove the pot from the heat. Strain into a bowl. Whisk in the bourbon. Refrigerate. Keeps about 4 days in the fridge.

Chocolate & Rum Dandy Drizzle

MAKES ABOUT 3 CUPS

1 cup heavy cream

1½ cups whole milk

2 cups dark chocolate, chopped

2½ tablespoons butter

1 tablespoon vanilla extract

3 tablespoons dark spiced rum, such as Kraken

⅛ teaspoon cinnamon

This cinnamon- and rum-scented chocolate sauce is thinner than hot fudge. It's perfect for drizzling over bowls of ice cream and sundaes.

1. Put the cream and milk in a small pot over medium heat. Heat it until it just starts to simmer, stirring occasionally. Remove from heat.
2. Toss in the chocolate and butter. Let sit for 5 minutes, then whisk until the chocolate has melted and the mixture is uniform. Whisk in the vanilla extract, dark rum, and cinnamon.
3. Cool to room temperature, then chill completely in the fridge. This will keep for about 2 weeks.

Homemade Maraschino Cherries

Sweet cherries, stemmed and pitted

Sugar

Maraschino liqueur

Yep, you can make these sweet little red babies at home. It takes about a week, but it's well worth the effort. Make as big a jar as you like. Here's the basic technique.

1. Loosely pack a clean mason jar with stemmed, pitted cherries.
2. Pour sugar into the jar, shaking it to distribute among the fruit. Use enough sugar so that the cherries are all thoroughly coated. Let it sit overnight on the counter to get lush and juicy.
3. Fill the jar with maraschino liqueur. Cap it tightly and give it a shake. Refrigerate for about a week, shaking the jar every day. Enjoy!

Don't Use Cheap Cherry Liqueur Normally, I say that substitutions are totally cool. Be careful with this one, though. Cheap cherry liqueur can taste like cough syrup. Make sure you use the good stuff for this one.

Index

About the Author

Jessie Cross runs The Hungry Mouse (*www.thehungry mouse.com*), a nationally recognized food blog known for its step-by-step recipes and high-quality photography.

A self-taught home cook, Jessie loves to help folks learn how to cook. Some of her favorite culinary moments include being one of fifteen bloggers invited to a *Bon Appétit* magazine bakeoff, developing recipes for Kraft and Pepperidge Farm, and being featured online in *Saveur, Better Homes & Gardens, Bon Appétit, iVillage, Serious Eats*, and *The Kitchn*. When she's not busy making ice cream or baking pies, she works as an ad agency creative type. Jessie lives in Salem, Massachusetts, with her husband and a small pack of very friendly wolves.